PRAISE FOR *OUTSIDE THE GATES*

"What happens when the angst of existentialism meets the agony of existence in a time of secular fundamentalist tyranny? William Hackett's thought-provoking novella, set against the backdrop of Nazi-occupied France during World War II, offers penetrating answers to this perennially relevant question."

— **JOSEPH PEARCE**, author of *Benedict XVI: Defender of the Faith*

"In a rich and intricate debut, Hackett combines the terrifying urgency of a WWII prisoner's escape with deep psychological and spiritual insight. The struggle of Jean Wahl will serve as a mirror into the reader's own complex humanity."

— **ELEANOR BOURG NICHOLSON**, author of *A Bloody Habit* and *Brother Wolf*

"*Outside the Gates* can only be described as a philosophical thriller. You can't put down Hackett's fast-paced story, based on true events, of Jean Wahl's harrowing escape from Nazi-occupied France. And you can't help but pick it up a second time, to meditate more slowly with Hackett's Wahl on the mysteries of life and death, of good and evil. This novel crackles with spiritual intensity. It is a transcendent debut in the fullest sense of the word."

— **STEVEN KNEPPER**, Virginia Military Institute

"Riveting and ruminative by turns, Hackett's novella immerses us in those most extraordinary moments of Jean Wahl's life, as the body and the soul of this celebrated French philosopher elude his Nazi captors. Every tense look can be felt in this hair-raising suspense novel, yet Hackett also raises our minds to what it means to live. Here we have one literary philosopher's remarkable tribute to another, and extraordinary white-knuckled spiritual reading for everyone else."

— **ROBERT WYLLIE**, Ashland University

OUTSIDE THE GATES

OUTSIDE the GATES

W.C. HACKETT

Angelico Press

First published in the USA
by Angelico Press 2021
Copyright © W. C. Hackett 2021

For information, address:
Angelico Press, Ltd.
169 Monitor St.
Brooklyn, NY 11222
www.angelicopress.com

ppr   978-1-62138-807-4
cloth   978-1-62138-808-1

Book and cover design
by Michael Schrauzer

The world is like the impression left by the telling of a story.

— Yoga Vasistha

TABLE OF CONTENTS

OUTSIDE THE GATES

Here you come across a fragment of a larger story in the middle of its telling. A few brief facts in order to gain some historical bearings: Jean Wahl was born on the 25th of May, 1888, the son of an English teacher. He was a philosopher and poet, in fact, one of the key figures of the existentialist movement. Like his uncle, Henri Bergson, he was a professor of philosophy at the Sorbonne. The events he recalls here took place when he was fifty-three years old. At this time he was still a bachelor, and was yet to have any children. At this time he was a "filthy Jew." At this time he suffered persecution, losing his position at the Sorbonne in the autumn of 1940 because of his Jewish ancestry. Over the months that followed he was summoned by SS *Hauptsturmführer* Theodor Dannecker, head of the Paris division of the *Judenreferat* (Office of Jewish Affairs) of the *Sicherheitsdienst* (Nazi Security Service), was arrested, tortured, and imprisoned, first at Paris's La Santé Prison, then at Drancy Internment Camp. As a result of several degrees of chance aligning with the daring machinations of members of the French Resistance, a nurse, his brother, former students . . . he escaped. These are historical facts. And there are many more, in the story told. But these, and these alone, are the ones for which I am willing to take responsibility. This is a work of fiction, after all. Besides, here, I am not the one telling the story. Like you, I am only an observer. As for the setting, the place of the telling, it is the same for every story:

to be human is to be in a place, however strange.

The fragment told here begins at the moment of escape, in early January 1942. Now Professor Wahl enters into hiding in Paris with another escapee, the deathly-ill Gilles Alain. Together they must reach the Free Zone in the south.

W. C. H.

1 | THE GATES

Where am I? — Ah yes: my words. These were the first words of my freedom. I shouted them: "We are free, Gilles Alain, we are free!" The pure elation of the escapee. One does not normally leave a Nazi prison camp under the watching eyes of the guards and a regiment of German soldiers. One does not normally escape from a Nazi prison camp at all. But there I was. I walked through the open gates.

Now, I did not tell you: before I had uttered those words of euphoria and surprise to Gilles Alain Badinter, shuffling down Avenue Henri Barbusse in a mass of desperately ill men, with the ringing metal of the closing of the gate of Drancy Internment Camp still in our ears, before we had passed onto Avenue Honorine, in fact, just as we were walking down Rue des Rosiers, and before even the gate of Drancy had disappeared behind the large building on the corner of Rosiers and Avenue Jean Jaurès, I turned my head to look back: I saw, in the foreground, the soldiers and guards dispersing, and, through the gate, the man with the megaphone climbing down the stairs of the platform.

In the background there roiled a dark sea, the assembly of the depressed, the persecuted, the suffering. There was no holy mountain in the shadow of which this Great Assembly gathered. They stood before a void of blackness. They gazed into the void, but without faces and without color: grey, cold, and though ranged together in numbers like loosely organized regiments, they were, each, alone. These prisoners stared at me with the face of a great emptiness. And my soul recoiled before them, as before a horrible enigma.

That day I left the prison camp that held me for three months. Somewhere on earth it was a day like any other. There, where I was, it was cold. There was no sun. A bitter wind stung my face and bit my gaunt body through my dirty, threadbare clothes. Stepping outside the gates of the Camp meant stepping into Paris. This was occupied Paris, mind you. A shadow of Paris. A gray, wintered Paris. Joyless Paris. What a contradiction in terms. A heavy, leaden sky crowded down on top of us. The streets were dirty. I remember this detail most clearly: the streets were just as dirty as the interior of the Camp. They were as dirty as our unwashed bodies. I should have understood what this meant. I felt that it meant something. But I confess to you: I still do not understand. Life speaks a language that is too big, too weighty, too ponderous and deep for any of us who live it. And it speaks this language not only in its suffering, but also in its joys. But even before that, behind both joy and suffering, life speaks this impenetrable, unfathomable language whenever and wherever it is: *life*. And maybe . . . I feel like I am nearly raving . . . maybe beyond joy and suffering there is a place, a place outside, where they join together and are wholly transcended by something terrible and unfathomable, something . . . Maybe we are nearly there . . . Or have we, have I only just begun the journey, just begun to open my eyes, even now, after all I have seen? After all I have done? All I have lived?

Gilles Alain and I walked through the gates of Drancy, together, with the eight hundred released prisoners. Gilles

Alain leaning like a leaden effigy on my arm. Gilles Alain was a walking death. He did not know it. Do the dying ever know it? It was as if the months of our suffering in the camp had blinded us to the severity of our sickness: dysentery, more or less untreated, is a deadly contagion. I felt this in myself and saw it in others' sunken black eyes. Yet just the night before in the darkness of my barracks, lying on the straw-strewn floor, I had somehow passed through the worst of that horrible illness. Health is a miracle. Like all miracles, one does not experience its miraculous character except, first, when it is gone, in its horrible absence, and second, when and if one is lucky enough to experience its restoration. And then the fragmented agony of illness becomes the dream, an unreality, a memory.

I was weak and hollowed out, but a distant echo of the crisp bell of health was already ringing in my chest that morning. Looking back, I do not know how we managed — all those sick men — to wander through the gates. We did not understand at the time what was happening. We assembled before our barracks; our names were called; the gates opened; we left. The Nazis bled the polluted vein of sickness into the City. They could not risk contaminating their many barracks of soldiers housed next door to the Camp. — Am I repeating myself? Forgive me if I am already repeating myself. Well, how pleased I am to have the opportunity now to resume my story. I began telling it so very long ago, and in quite another place . . . Yes, hold my hand; it gives me strength. You are so quiet and attentive. Love, how strong it is. Stronger than —

2 | THE FORT, AND GILLES ALAIN'S STORY

Death is a sharp iron that cleaves without mercy. Our numbers diminished as we walked. We drifted, numbly, through the cold streets of northeast Paris. I never noticed where they went, our wandering, dying fellows, peeling off in twos or threes into cafes or groceries or side streets, perhaps to attempt a phone call or to rest behind a building or to find a friend, someone with a bed in which they could wake from this nightmare, or someone with a car to take them away, to the south, into free France.

We, Gilles Alain and I, kept moving. But eventually, without thought, we too peeled off from the group, making a sharp right off of Avenue Henri Barbusse into the capillaries of Paris: with every step we took we moved farther away from Drancy; with every step the more we feared returning there. "We could be chased down or picked up again: what if the Germans change their minds?" We spoke with hushed voices, as if every person on the street were an ear of the enemy. "What if our release were part of some training exercise devised by that man, by Dannecker, for their hunters to track us on the streets of Paris?"

The name Dannecker made me shudder.

I turned, with violence and a sick terror grasping my chest, to look behind me. I half expected to see his sinister, birdlike visage and to feel his clenched gloved fist strike my face. Yet every time I turned, there was only an empty street. "Berlin. He was recalled to Berlin," whispered Gilles Alain weakly. "He will return, and we will meet him when we least expect it," I said in reply. We turned off the main street, but we continued to move both south and west. After a couple hours of walking, Gilles Alain grew tired. He said nothing but his weight on my arm grew until I was struggling to hold him up. I, too, was weak.

We stopped, by necessity, to rest among the small forest of trees around the Fort d'Aubervilliers. The fort, built one hundred years previously by Adolph Thiers to control the city's insurrections, was now occupied by the Germans. We could not stay long. But the forest itself seemed unpatrolled. It was in fact quite desolate, which is what drew us to it.

Reaching the fort, we knew we were a cannonball's distance from the old city of Paris. Underneath the dormant, leafless trees we wandered for a few minutes. I learned a lot about my new companion in suffering, Gilles Alain, in those few minutes: both of his parents were orphaned as newborns by the 1832 cholera epidemic; they were raised by two adjoining families in Le Marais, under the shadow of the synagogue at 10 rue Pavée. He had studied law and architecture at university but returned to his adopted parents without completing his degree in order to run their kosher deli when his father turned ill. His father was an invalid for a year and then died. His adopted mother died shortly thereafter, from grief. They were childless but for Gilles Alain.

Gilles Alain had never married. He ran the deli until the day he was stopped by a German officer as he exited the door of the shop, also the front door of his apartment, on Saturday, on his way to synagogue. The officer asked to be served lunch. Gilles Alain told him the deli was closed. He gruffly forced Gilles Alain back through the door and sat down at a table, demanding to be served *boudin noir aux pommes*. Gilles Alain was terrified, and said, in a trembling voice, that "no blood sausage could be found in this store or this neighborhood." The officer stood, grabbed Gilles Alain, and threw him into a shelf. All its contents — cans, bottles, bags of bread, olive oil tins — spilling on top of him or breaking on the floor. When Gilles Alain opened his eyes, he saw that two more men in uniform had entered the deli. With small black clubs they denuded the remaining shelves, overturned tables, and broke the glass cases.

When the two thugs went upstairs to the apartment, the officer, who had returned to his seat, revived his original demand, and asked to be served "this establishment's most famous dish." Gilles Alain rushed into the kitchen and began shakily preparing his own Sabbath day's meal of *boeuf consommé*, *foie gras*, meatballs in Bourguignon sauce and schalet pudding. He was weeping. The officer reviled him from time to time. Above his head he could hear the men furiously trashing his apartment. All he could think of was his mother's crystal glasses in the mahogany *vaisselier* opposite the piano. When he heard the *vaisselier* crash to the floor his tears stopped. He brought out the food and carefully placed it before the officer, who sat, staring at Gilles Alain with a look of contempt, hands folded under his chin. Gilles Alain stood for some minutes under the officer's cold gaze until an idea flashed in his mind: wine! The officer is waiting for a drink! Gilles Alain ran to the kitchen and fetched a bottle of burgundy from the back of the wine cupboard — a *Bourgogne Chablis Grand Cru*, the most expensive wine in his possession, for which he was permanently awaiting an occasion to drink. He should have thought to run out of the back alley door. Why had he not? He returned to the officer with the bottle, poured him a glass and took a step back. Holding the glass of wine in his left hand, the officer stretched out his right hand and, with a swift movement, swept the entire meal off the table, sending it crashing onto the floor. He took a sip of the wine, and, with exaggerated manners, sat it back in its place on the table. Immediately Gilles Alain heard the men descending the back stairs from the apartment. He did not turn around. There was something horrible, something unspeakable in the officer's gaze.

And the officer's face was the last thing he saw. Gilles Alain woke up in the back seat of a car, slumped forward. He dared not move. The officer seated beside him. That man who said nothing, but sat, silent, unmoving, stiff, like death's officer on holiday. The car stopped, the door was opened, and Gilles Alain was pulled by his collar out and onto the ground by a German soldier. When he staggered to his feet, he found himself standing at the front gate of Drancy. It was only then, he said, that he noticed the back of his head, wet with blood and pounding, pounding with pain. He never discovered why the Germans targeted him, but they seemed to be looking for something when they ransacked his store and apartment. What startled me most, however, was Gilles Alain's description of the officer: he mentioned only his brown leather gloves and his terrible, empty eyes . . .

I did not ask, and Gilles Alain never said the officer's name. He did not have to.

3 | A DECISION, AND BREAD

I left Gilles Alain beneath the veining ash branches of a towering *platane* tree. It was under a *platane* that Hippocrates taught his students the medical arts on the Greek island of Kos. These trees can live for thousands of years. I told this to Gilles Alain who smiled absently and drifted off to sleep, oblivious to the world around him. Like a child, I thought. Leaving him, I wandered among the trees of the Fort thinking about what to do next. This was the first time since the gates of Drancy that I truly felt the winter's cold. It was now January — I told you this, no? — and the wind was bitter: within the gates, as a captive, I had never felt the cold of winter as I did at that moment. Of course, I always felt cold there, day and night. At Drancy one could never quite get warm. But never the cold of exposure as I felt it among the trees of the Fort d'Aubervilliers. Maybe the tall walls of Drancy's three sides somehow isolated us from the winds of winter. Or maybe our first taste of freedom also woke us anew to the basic human needs that were now back in our control — the need for shelter and protection. Maybe freedom woke us again in a different way to the fragility of our embodied existence than did that long, empty episode of subject imprisonment, the effects of which still ruled so powerfully over our minds and bodies. Captivity gave us shelter, but it was not of the kind that we had forged for ourselves: it was forced on us. I remember thinking that Gilles Alain and I were like the first hominids millennia ago that ventured out of the protecting trees and onto the savannah, naked and exposed. What lay ahead? Whatever it was, it was crouching in the shadows, waiting to devour us. Snow began to fall.

We could not sleep on the streets. And we could not make it out of Paris without help. The train stations would be monitored by German troops, the streets by French *gendarmeries*. And my experience at prison and the camp, run by French police under the administration of German military, showed how much my fellow countrymen could be trusted. I still marvel at how quickly peace can turn to war, safety to terror, civilization to chaos . . .

It was decided. We would go into hiding in Paris therefore and organize an escape from the city into the *zone libre*. We, Gilles Alain and I, would flee to Mâcon. My brother would give Gilles Alain shelter, just as he would take me in, just as he had taken in my parents when the Germans first invaded Paris. Yes, Gilles Alain, the orphan, would be a part of our family now. And I would reestablish my life in nearby Lyon until the end of this occupation, until the end of this war. I had plenty of contacts at the Université de Lyon — having taught there in the years '33 – '36 — and Gilles Alain . . . we could find him something to do. But he is still very sick; we will have to convalesce somewhere safe . . . But where? Where should we go? As I was thinking these thoughts I began to feel weak and dizzy. Just as the cold wounded me differently outside of the camp, as a free man, so did hunger: my stomach bawled and terrorized me: a free man should not be hungry. A prisoner expects it.

I found myself on the edge of the wood staring across Avenue Jean Jaurès. A *boulangerie-pâtisserie* on the corner. Windows glowing with golden warmth. A tingling sensation at the bottom of my chest reminding me of my childhood. Seeing no uniforms on the road, I crossed the street.

At the window I saw first the heaping baskets of bread on shelves behind the counter. Loaves were thrown, higgledy-piggledy, above two glass cases crammed with assortments of pastries. I entered. No customers, no *boulanger* or *maître-pâtissier* sitting on the old wooden stool beside the brick oven. The oven door was open: a glowing hardwood fire was burning inside. There were no flames, only coals consumed with heat; breathing bright red, orange and white. The *pâtissier* must have stepped out for a moment, perhaps, I thought, for an *apéritif* or an *espresso* next door. . . I walked up to the glass cases and drew in this little universe's breath of life. The fiery warmth, the smell of fresh bread, the colors and textures of the junkily ordered confections — sticky *tarte tatin*, simultaneously delicate and hardy *profiterole*, the thin chocolate disks of the *mendiants* studded with colorful nuts and fruit, square and cylindrical *petit fours* of exquisite combinations of flavor and color — a row of blue, a row of red, a row of pink with green square tops, a row of dark brown with marbled bodies. . . Next to these a fantastically large plate supported a small hill of *macarons*, and, beside them, *madeleines* roughly gathered like a child's collection of seashells, densely coated éclairs, *pan au chocolat* . . . The lavish opulence roiled around me like a sea. The contrast of this urbane paradise with the winter world outside could not have been more pronounced. I was nearly sick. Yet at the next moment I felt something within that had long disappeared, something high and human, something foreign, esoteric like the taste of fine wine. Human culture, that miraculous capacity for progressively unfolding nature's peculiar inexhaustibility, that innocent perversity, discovered me again. It rests directly on top of our animal natures: our animal selves inhabit culture like the slimy snail in its shell.

My feet found the floor. On top of the narrow shelf next to the oven was the *pâtissier's* wide wooden peel, ancient and possessing a thick crack running the entirety of its long slender handle. Its two fragments were bound along its length by heavy metal clasps bent around its circumference. This handle, worn smooth by decades of use, lay across the aisle between the oven and the glass case before me.

And sitting on the peel — *mon Dieu* ! A round loaf the size of my torso. It was steaming. Its mass and density drew all things in the little shop around it in untroubled orbit.

The loaf was flat on the bottom, domed on top; its thick, crackled crust peppered with white-yellow flour. I saw the *pâtissier's* firm hands, his artisan fingers, white sleeves rolled up to the elbow, folding and punching, turning and pressing the dough, waiting for the subtle changes in its consistency to tell him that this romance of pressure and soft resistance had accomplished its purpose. The textured ridges from his impassioned scoring made a beautiful pattern of irregular diamonds over the loaf's domed surface. Faintest curls of steam rose from the center of the loaf. It was hard, crispy on the outside, but — I felt this within myself — heavy with warmth in its heart. Warm bread: this enchanted me. I reached out my hand, placing it gently on the counter. A certain charge in my spine told me that the tip of my finger had grazed the end of the peel's narrow handle before resting on the glass case. I found myself pressing the meaty edge of my hand below the pinky finger along the peel's rounded handle. Sliding my hand over the top and then wrapping my fingers gently around it, I imagined (did I?) that the peel still possessed a trace of the warmth from the fleshy hand of the baker. This did not alarm me. I pulled the peel several inches to myself, being careful not to pull it too far, and, leaning on the glass, I stretched forward and wrapped my other hand further down the handle. Then, lifting it with both hands . . . I realized how weak I had become: my arms trembled under its oblong and awkward weight. The dense loaf on its paddle swayed and then danced before me. Panicking, I yanked it towards myself with all the power in my arms. The paddle twisted and the bread fell on the floor with a soft thud. Stung by an electric shock, I walked around and behind the glass case, stepped over the bread and turned around. The warmth of the oven on my face and hands. I paused and bent over, slid my fingers underneath the loaf's sides, gripping it with my thumbs. Between my hands, the life within the bread electrified the crisp crust and pulsated through my arms, tingling my scalp. I pulled the loaf to my chest and straightened up. I closed my eyes, raised it to my nose and pressed it to my lips. I inhaled. Sourdough. Salt and honey . . .

My exotic reverie was short lived. From far away I heard it, muffled, like a foreign hand passing through thick layers of drapery to grab me. Between my shoulder blades I felt the unmistakable presence of a man's harsh gaze.

I turned.

He stood in the doorway. How clearly my eye still sees him. His hands: baker's chubby. Healthy red lips snarling from under a deep brown moustache hung on a flat face. His dark figure stood frozen against a dull white background, startled in the very act of placing his baker's *toque blanche* on his head.

His bleached double-breasted jacket was open at the top; its knotted cloth buttons discolored by the oil of stubby fingers. The uppermost button hung by a thread.

I opened my mouth. He opened his. Neither spoke. His eyes narrowed and he placed his hands on his hips. In the face of this Parisian *boulanger* flashed the harsh guards at Drancy. His cold eyes pinned me as if to a corner as he lowered his chin. Yet the gravity of the bread in my arms retained a greater orbital power. I walked around the counter like a cat, and, again, stopped. I do not know why, but at that moment, an extravagant grin spread across my face. I crossed the shop with an alien deliberateness and stopped only about a half step from him. He was a large man, fleshy and vigorous. Heat radiated from his body. I raised my eyes to meet his. His breath tasted my glassy forehead. His silvery eyes searched my face.

It was as if in the flash of that moment my soul was bared. It was as if this *boulanger* saw what there was to read within — all of my suffering, all of my hunger, all of my sickness, the hatred that had been heaped over me since my arrest. His nose twitched. Eyes softened. Startling myself, I said: "Monsieur: excuse me. This is the bread of the people of France." With Parisian deliberateness he stepped to the side. I walked through the door and onto the street.

Outside, in the winter air, I took a deep breath and looked down: between my arms, clasped to my chest was a revelation and life.

I half-ran back to Gilles Alain. His face, his arms, his legs and torso were covered with a light layer of snow. He looked like a dead man. His cheeks and lips were a faint blue; the skin around his eyes was a translucent white. He was a stone angel that might be seen in a cemetery, forever melting in the rain. I sat down beside him. Rousing him with eager violence, I broke the bread. In a single movement he sat up, extended his hands forward like a begging child and tore a large chunk of bread, stuffing the whole in his mouth. Pulling it out a little he began to suck on the bread as if he had no teeth. His mouth was dry. He wept and said he could not taste the bread. Watching him, I raised the remainder of the loaf to my mouth. Beyond the crisp crust the bread still traced its warmth. I will never forget its taste. The bread was freedom. It strengthened me. As hungry as he was, Gilles Alain could only swallow a few bites. He could not salivate and waves of nausea tamped down the mounting flame of his appetite.

The little bit of nourishment we received somehow awoke us to the cold. How stiff my legs were; my hands and feet were wet, already dully burning again from the cold.

Without a word we rose to our feet and began to walk.

4 | SOUP, AND THE SOUL OF FRANCE

A thick blanket of snow muffled the city. The street sighed its loneliness. Standing under the lamplight on Rue des Beaux Arts, I looked up at the hotel façade. My head was heavy and alien to me. How many times I had stood just here, smoking my pipe after a long, wine-soaked dinner with friends, before entering my rooms in the hotel! How different the street felt now. The rhythmic appearance of our breath vaporizing before us in the lamplight was the only movement in the picture; the only sound was my heavy breathing. Gilles Alain was panting, near imperceptibly, at my side. He was hunched over, grasping his stomach with one hand while the other hung at his side, the backs of his fingers grazing the surface of the snow. It cost him much, but he looked up at me and smiled. No window in the building betrayed any light although it was only eight o' clock in the evening. Examining the edifice, I let out an awkward moan of relief: my window shades were not drawn. I had decided that if the Nazis were there lying in wait for us, they would have drawn the shades.

We entered. Gilles Alain's strength had now evaporated, as if on reaching our destination he left every last bit of energy outside in the cold. I was carrying him now. We passed through the small entry of the hotel. Its internal doors were closed but unlocked: in ordinary times they would always be left open: a compromise between the suspicion and unease accompanying occupation and the stubborn demand for normalcy; an act of subtle defiance. The circular lobby held the hotel together like an atom's nucleus; the bar and dining room, straight ahead, offices and reception to the left, a wide stair to the right. It was, to our unadjusted eyes, absent of all light and all welcome. By the force of forgotten habit I turned to the left. Through open doors and across a broad room: a single candle burned atop the concierge's desk. And behind it, softly glowing, the gentle face of a man floated in the darkness. It was Louis-Baptiste David. "He is still here," I thought. I wondered at the realization. The continuity with a former world comforted me.

Louis-Baptiste's face rested sleepily between his hands. As we approached through the darkness, our wet feet squeaking painfully on the polished floor, he did not move. The light from the candle danced sharply in his eyes; eyes expressionless, eyes of observation traced our path across the room. The wind from outside made the candle dance as we lumbered towards him. The external front door of the hotel slammed shut on its hinge, and the candle blew out. Gilles Alain and I stopped, cold in the darkness. There was no sound. A match flared excitedly in Louis-Baptiste's hands and relit the candle. We resumed our slow procession. Louis-Baptiste dropped from his swivel stool behind the desk and erected himself as we drew near. He peered at two dark visitors without curiosity or fear. He was a small man, even smaller than I, and his height was greater sitting in the stool than it was standing. As it was now, his hands, grasping the thick edge of the desk in front of him, were resting, almost like a giant cat's paws, just below his chin. Gilles Alain and I entered the brown light. Louis-Baptiste's large eyes stared out at us in dumb dis-animation. I spoke:

"*Pardonnez-moi, monsieur, mais j'ai perdu mon clé à nouveau* . . ."

Louis-Baptiste's chubby face dropped the mask of unrecognition to reveal the rapt picture of an innocent child. "*Monsieur! Monsieur!* . . . *Monsieur! Monsieur!*," he exclaimed in erupting bursts of frivolity. "*Monsieur! Mon* . . ." It was as if the boy had rediscovered a dear but forgotten plaything.

Louis-Baptiste would have repeated this song, I imagine, indefinitely unless I had spoken: "*Monsieur le concierge*," I sang, surprising myself at the vigor of my voice, "give me the pleasure of introducing to you my dear friend, Monsieur Gilles Alain Badinter, a chef and shopkeeper from Le Marais . . ."

Gilles Alain bowed his head. Louis-Baptiste David waggled and reached out his hand. He was nearly jumping up and down as he shook the feeble and frozen hand of Gilles Alain. "*Mais Monsieur, mon professeur*, they said you . . . I was told that . . ." He paused and then continued, "But here you are. I am so happy to see you." He clasped his hands together and drew them playfully to his cheek. "I have not . . . your rooms . . . your home has not been touched. No one has been here." He dropped his hands and his voice changed into a whispered temperamental growl: "I mean, they have not come here." Then his voice changed again, dropping to an animated whisper. "But there are, yes, let me see, several letters for you; several letters in fact, from your friends and also not a few students — my how they do adore you! — they have come calling and left messages or notes, and a few sealed letters. Look, yes, here they are. And I . . . let me think . . ." (rubbing an eyebrow with the side of his finger) "Yes, the key, you have 'misplaced.' Misplaced indeed! Professor Wahl — the key to your apartment. And now, I hope I have not misplaced the hotel's copy . . ." As Louis-Baptiste fumbled in the drawer of his desk, Gilles Alain slouched further.

With a mild moan, he fell to the ground, turning, and like a drunk man pressed his back against the front of the desk. He struggled to catch his breath. Louis-Baptiste did not seem to notice, but found the key that opens the box in the storeroom and ran off with the candle, through the doorway and across the lobby to the office of the superintendent behind the stairs. I turned and slid down the side of the concierge's desk beside Gilles Alain. His head was bowed, and his chin was resting on his chest. His breathing was labored. I could hear Louis-Baptiste singing and talking to himself as he moved about, the glow of the candle rising and falling through the doorway to my left. In the window at my right, I watched the snow, falling like blankets through the lamplight.

Louis-Baptiste soon returned holding a tray. He approached and crouched down. On the tray was the candle, the key, a bottle of wine and two glasses. His eyes were dancing in the light: "I have awakened Madame David. She is very happy you are here. Oh so happy. She is warming up some *daube de boeuf*, no, *la garbure landaise*, yes, for you and Monsieur your friend . . . Mon Dieu! He is asleep . . . No doubt very tired, very tired indeed. Come, we must rouse him. We must get you to your rooms. We must light a fire." Louis-Baptiste handed me the tray. He wrapped his powerful little arms around Gilles Alain's haggard body, raising him to his feet. We ascended the stairs slowly. Passing through the hallways of my floor, we approached the figure of Madame David standing beside the door, wrapped in a blanket and holding a candle. Her nightcap was on her head but its thick red string was untied and hanging down the sides of her face. A few wiry curls of hair were slipping out of the cap above her temples. She was as short as Louis-Baptiste, but wider. The joy manifest in her toothy smile and chubby lips made her appear less porcine than I remembered but just as innocent and amiable as her husband.

"OK, woman, thank you, yes, yes, here he is . . ." said Louis-Baptiste shifting his glance back and forth between her and me, comically changing his expression from sternness to apology as his head turned.

Madame David broke in: "*Monsieur le professeur! Bienvenue à votre maison!* Welcome! Welcome! . . . Welcome! Welcome!," with the same sing-song tenor as her husband. The blanket dropped from her shoulders. The sleeves of her nightdress were rolled up, exposing plump red arms waving joyously.

Louis-Baptiste jumped forward and grabbed the key from the tray in my hands. Pressing it into the lock and opening the door, he said: "We must let them rest, woman. Their journey has exhausted them."

Madame David nodded her head in knowing agreement. She caught Gilles Alain in her arms as he parted from Louis-Baptiste's side, staggered and half-fell forward. "Oh dear, this one is quite ill: he is burning up!" she exclaimed as she carried him into my foyer on her arm. Together Monsieur and Madame David led Gilles Alain to the bedroom and laid him on the bed. I removed his shoes and covered him with a blanket. He was shivering.

"He needs a nurse," said Madame David matter-of-factly. She warmed me with her look of motherly concern. I had not seen, had not *felt* such a look for so long. I spoke:

"There cannot be any . . . but there must be . . . You see, Madame David, we must take precautions, we must be careful about who knows we are here. But I think I can find a nurse, and a doctor, but . . ."

"Nonsense," she exclaimed, placing her hands on her hips. "I will nurse this poor man back to health. I will clean your clothes, which have seen better days, and I, well . . . *you*, Monsieur Wahl, you must clean yourself immediately." Madame David chuckled. "Come, let me draw you a bath. And I will find some more blankets for your friend. Leave your clothes just inside the door. I will return tomorrow morning . . ."

Madame David bustled around my apartment, straightening, stopping, rushing to the bathroom, turning at the door, taking a step, turning again, entering the bathroom, starting the water, splashing her hand in it. She was humming and talking to herself just as Louis-Baptiste had done earlier. They seemed to me to have aged considerably since I was gone. "Oh my, dear me," she exclaimed, rushing out of the bathroom, "I nearly forgot! Your supper! Your stew is on the kettle!" She lumbered forward and Louis-Baptiste bowed low. They turned and walked out the door, Madame David first.

"Soup is coming! Soup is coming!" sang Madame David in a half whisper. She snapped her fingers and trundled down the hallway, Louis-Baptiste in her train. I closed the door and took off my coat and jacket. Pulling the small lunchtin from Drancy out of the flap pocket of my jacket, I placed it on the kitchen table next to the government issued gas mask that was staring at me from out of its forest green tin, its lid lying beside, just where I had placed it in the world before my arrest. A lunchtin, issued at the Camp, sitting together with the government-issued gas mask. Nourishment, if you could call it that, provided by the Nazis and protection from their bombs of nerve gas, provided by the French government. I could have laughed at the irony, but I didn't. The words from the Mishnah I had inscribed into the lunchtin glowed on its

surface: *we-'al korchakha attah chay*: "despite yourself, you live."
These words . . .

I placed the coat over Gilles Alain, who was again asleep. Then
I walked to the bathroom to finish drawing the bath.

I took off my clothes.

5 | THE VISION

In the mirror was a man. "Death warmed up" as the soldiers in the trenches say to one another. I did not know this man. He spoke. His words were strange but they felt — I feel — as if they were a key. And if only I knew where to place the key. But I did — I do — not. He spoke in hieroglyphs.

"What is a dream?" He demanded a response.

I could not answer, shocked, as I was, into a deranged silence.

The man smiled. "This question is impossible to answer," he said. "For even if the dreamer knows that he is dreaming, this knowledge, this awakening as it were, is only an element within the dream. It, too, is illusion, composed wholly of dream material. Even in dreams there is much reality. Reality, one could say, is the very stuff of dreams. Dreams are not reality, and yet reality is all they are. Dreams are the falsehood, one could say, of reality . . ."

The man's words were cold and clear, like the depths of water bending tree limbs that fall into them. He continued: "To awaken is to pass from sleep to another state, it is to pass from one world to another. Which way does the waking go? Which world is the false pendant of the other? Who can decide between them?"

The man gazed at me, a mocking look in his eyes:

"When I open my eyes to feel the weight of my body pressing me, holding me, riveting me to this heavy, fragile world of struggle and death, of ignorance and endless frenzy and distraction, am I awake? Or does the waking go in the other direction, through the dream, beyond forgetting and the wall of silence, into the dreamless, into what is real? Who can decide between them?"

A sudden urge to run gripped me, to hide from the face in the mirror and the wild words it spoke. But I could not move; neither could I turn my head or close my eyes. "I don't know," I stammered. The man smiled again, with a far off look that seemed to scorn contemptuously any wisdom humanity might have ever claimed for itself:

"Your old teacher, Socrates, on his deathbed told the friends gathered around him that sleeping and waking are opposites, and like hot and cold, high and low, are derived from one another: what is cold is 'cold' only relative to 'hot'; whatever sleep is, I only know it relative to waking life . . . You only know you are 'awake' because you know what it is to be asleep. Our knowledge is ignorance because stuck within this vicious, inescapable cycle of opposites derived from each other."

The dark face paused, cackled, and, after a rapt quiet, continued: "But there is some hope, that god-appointed wise man said. Some things, even within the leaden world of ignorance and illusion, appear to come from elsewhere. Virtue, for example, is different: true courage is not derived from fear (as when fear of dying leads to so-called 'courage' in the camp). True courage comes when bodied life is no longer held onto as something important, when death is no longer feared as your adversary . . . as your hunter."

With those words I quaked, but he took no notice:

"Virtue. Ha! Maligned and misunderstood! As if it were something trivial, something easy to find, as if it were not the most desirable possibility of all mankind! Something just faintly reached in the dark worlds of deepest human dreams that has, for some unfathomable purpose, invaded the so-called waking world of your paltry struggle and survival.

"The buried virtue of your ancients' ancients is only uncovered by a cultivated awareness, knowledge of a peculiar kind, knowledge of our essential ignorance, which Socrates called 'wisdom.' This knowledge is reasoned reflection on the state of illusion that is ours in the world, leading to the stunning recognition that the truth, the unfathomable truth, alone really is. The truth that is beyond our labyrinth of circles, unreachable, hidden, but at the same time everywhere, immediate, like the light that is too bright to look at but illumines all things. Everything derives from it, everything points to it, everything hides it!

"The one in single-hearted pursuit of ignorance, of the acceptance and affirmation of things as they are, the one who accepts the straight fact that the circle of opposites rules over us: this is the one who already begins to escape the labyrinth, to live bodied life in another, peculiar way. He awakens to the knowledge, in other words, that he is dreaming.

"Birth and death derive from one another. Both are within the dream. Both are subject to suffering, to the domination of desire for control, survival, and escape: the body is born; the body survives if chance allows it; the body dies. The self, the soul, is what awakens, but not in the body. The soul awakens when the body sleeps. Sleep is like death, a passage into another state . . .

"*And the body* . . . the body suffers. How it suffers! The body is dream-reality. The self, the soul is not. There is reality, but this dream is not it. There is reality, and it is the source of the dream, the illusion. To awaken, to leave the body in its sleep, is to be released from 'life,' to pass through the gates, to pass from the illusion of life, which is really death to life, which only appears as death within the dream. The dream-self, the body, once unlocked and opened, is left behind. It has performed its only *real* function: to swing open as a gate. And the gate is death, the death of illusion. The dreamer cannot awaken himself. He is awoken by another, from the other side, from the waking world. And when he is undergoing the process of awakening, the other appears veiled within the dream, first, not even as an alien element, but so well masked that he is not even recognized. But somehow the recognition happens: this is life acknowledging itself through death, reality becoming aware of itself through dream.

"Outside the gates: a world as different from this one as sleep is from what we call waking here, within them. Or so I have come to think."

The man stopped speaking. Something broke above my head or behind my eyes. Minutes passed. When I looked again, the vision had faded and in the mirror only darkness and my unfamiliar form. What was this bizarre reverie? The crystalline vision found the farthest reaches of the mind, a doorway of understanding opened only by trial and pain. I would not have recognized myself there, in the mirror, cold and skeletal, brow darkened by suffering, if it were not for the warm light of Monsieur and Madame David's kindness, hovering like a halo around a black void. I thought of them. They, in their generous simplicity — they are the soul of France. Her only hope . . . I looked on them, sleeping in their beds, at peace in a simplicity and wholeness riding on rafts of ignorance on the surface of an endless sea of chaos and unknown . . . I fell back into my bodied self and woke, terrified, as if fighting to escape a dream only to enter darkness.

I came to myself with a start, lying in the tub. The water was cold.

My madly thumping heart.

Emerging from the bathroom, I registered something for the first time: I was home. For all those months, everything inside my hotel apartment remained just as I had left it: in disarray. My books and papers along the shelved walls, stacked on tables and chairs. My American whiskey collection burning silently in its cabinet beside the grandfather clock. I would look into that tomorrow . . . I almost chuckled to myself at the thought. In the morning I am a prisoner of a Nazi internment camp and here I am, hours later, stretching out my legs in my own hotel apartment: fire glowing in the corner and two large bowls of *garbure*, ham preserved *en confit*, stale bread on the table. Glancing around the room, and, in fact, seeing no rabbi present, I ate. Though alone, I heartily performed the *chabrot*, pouring the dinner's red wine into the broth after eating the ham and vegetables out of both bowls. I savored long gulps of the mixture, bowl raised to my lips.

Body clean, stomach full. Gifts not to be measured . . . Minutes later, I fell asleep on my psychoanalyst's couch beside the window. A heavy wet snow, still falling.

6 | INSCAPE

I see where I am. Sunday morning. My first morning of freedom. Though I feel you, I do not see you. The room: heavy and dark. My heart racing painfully. My opened eyes. Thin rays of light radiating from beneath two drawn curtains, their organic patterns dancing vertically in the darkness. Struggling to still my spasmodic chest, to catch my breath. The heavy rug draped over my body as I lay, riveted to the brown leather of my psychoanalyst's couch. All was far away; all is far away. . .

(The spaces fanning around me)

◆ ◆ ◆

Morning's sunlight illuminating the leaden carpet that covers a wide raised dais running the length of the rectangular room, cutting it into two equal lengthwise halves. Beyond it — remaining in the half of the room where I lay suspended — at the far end, there would be one who stepped down to a fireplace in which red embers glow and up to which two wingback chairs are intimately pulled. Between the windows along the wall: an antique writing desk stacked haphazardly with books and papers. A small ladder-back chair pushed against the desk at a pleasing angle. In the interior of the room two pairs of narrow Italian red limestone *rosso levanto* columns at matching ends are set, ancient and stubborn, into the edge of the dais. This further helps, I observe, to separate one half

29

of the room from the other. The other half is darkened and still, shaded softly into a gray that feels like easy longing.

Sliding off the dais, I float into the sleeping gray, I feel below — I do not know how — two worn afghan rugs of equal size filling its entire length and separating it into two parts, repeating at ninety degrees the first division. This order pleases me. Each part of this half-division repeats the other half: the far half has two doors on both of its walls, both hinged, like Siamese twins, onto the same corner. The first door, on the long wall opposite the windows, is the entry. It opens out into the hallway and into another world. The second door beside it, sharing the short wall with the fireplace, enters the bedroom. The bedroom is filled by a large bed with a padded headboard of Tyrian purple velvet. In the bed there sleeps a man. I see him but, for the moment, I do not know his name. This does not disturb me. And though he sleeps, he appears both ill and exhausted. His exhaustion is not merely that of his illness, but something more. I see that I share that exhaustion with him. And I love him as I contemplate the weak fragility of his body burning beneath the sheets. Above his head there is raised an opulent oil painting in a spare, golden frame: a French cardinal of the imperial court in flowing scarlet robes. The cardinal is captured in mid-movement, bending dramatically on one knee, his arms slightly raised before him in elegant piety. His face: gazing into an unseen light that bathes his body in a dark room, it evinces contemplative ecstasy. He never moves; he never turns to look at me . . .

At the bedroom window: two neoclassical chairs overly padded on the arms and seat. They are covered with rich stripes of red, green and soft gold. The chairs share a small table of intricate woodwork composed of two levels and with a built-in double lamp on top from which hang two long pull chains with brass balls on the end.

On the wall beside the external door of the apartment an oval mirror hovers in a heavy square mahogany frame that resembles flames of fire in its corners. It flies in place above an antique drawered table. Beside the table is a diminutive chair that only children can sit in comfortably. It is unceremoniously stacked with faded books. The near part-half of the gray room beyond the columns also has a door on its small side, the mirror-image of the bedroom door. This door enters the *salle de bains*.

The *salle de bains* is not ornate. There is a cast iron clawfoot tub standing beside a sink with a small mirror. A man in an ill-fitting suit stands in the mirror. He is wearing a gas mask. He stares and points at me. He is laughing.

◆ ◆ ◆

I sat up on the couch. The imaginal spaces through which I had passed were like a face from childhood. I could dimly see, beyond the *rosso levanto* columns closest to me, rows of books stashed on their cherry wood shelves like a farmer's stone wall. My books. My apartment. I was aware enough of myself to remain content, half-immersed in that brackish state where the river of consciousness flowed back and forth with the ocean of the subconscious, waters arbitrarily reversing course but bearing even on their surface some incomprehensible higher meaning that has its home there in dream.

In the light and shadow of a Sunday morning, the foreignness of a familiar room engulfed me — those things, that space, they startled me as their light familiarity fell into place around me. Aided by the trials of the last months, I fell back into my pillow, the currents of mind carrying me again into the dreamscape. My eyes, half-opened in the still light, the cool warmth of sleep creeping and receding over me like tides. The contrasts of the room deepened. It became dramatic, opulent, and antique. I felt again the cozy weight of the large, folded rug covering me. And then, I heard it: the music that had carried me all along through the apartment in dream — one of Verdi's operas . . . *Rigoletto*: the horns! Filling the room like water in a porcelain tub.

My Sonorette radio player. And directly beneath the chandelier on the middle of the settee: someone sitting, unthinking, still. Madame David, not unlike a permanent but eccentric installment in the apartment. She was knitting, still amidst the slow rise and fall of uncountable fragments of light dancing in the sliced streams of white morning sun, shafting through the center of the maladjoined curtains. I sat up, less alarmed than baffled. She saw that I stirred, leapt forward, and threw back the heavy curtains. The pure virgin light of a new day flooded the room. Despite myself I smiled. I rose from my chair and wrapped myself in the bathrobe draped over the back of the Louis XV armchair rolled up to my couch from its regular place against the wall. Madame David reached out her chubby arm and led me by the hand across the room. We stepped down from the dais before the glowing fireplace. I sat in my old reading wing chair that had been pulled up to the fire. She poured tea into a dainty cup and saucer on the lampstand. The tea steamed wrathfully. We did not speak.

The fire dimmed. Madame David stooped down and stirred the coals. With her back to me she said: "He is still sleeping."

My mind returned, heavy with the recent past. The man in my bed: Gilles Alain.

The previous day struck me with a vicious blow: the gates of Drancy, the streets of Paris, Fort d'Aubervilliers, the bakery, snow, hunger, cold. German soldiers, occupation, starvation, disease, war. My mind crawled into the coals that Madame David stirred into life. I was alive but that was no comfort: I had much to fear.

Madame David placed in my hands a large stack of letters and messages that had accumulated since my arrest, carefully preserved by Louis-Baptiste. After she left to have a breakfast prepared by the hotel chef, I separated the letters from the folded messages. I examined the messages first. Most were from students and colleagues. Many asked if I could contact them that they may relay some news of special urgency. I could feel the hurried concern that ran through their words. The Occupation had made all of us more helpless, more fragile — pathetic, one could say, but at the same time determined, like children. The letters were more substantial: several from my family in Lyon, signed by my brother and father, which I read with some emotion. I had seen a few of the letters before: Paul always sent one copy of each letter he wrote to Santé or Drancy and to my apartment.

7 | A MEMORY, AND YOUR
INTERJECTION

The letter at the bottom of the pile I remember the most vividly. It was from a dear friend in Lyon, François Houng. François was not his given name: he assumed it when he came to France from China on a scholarship attached to the Institut franco-chinois de Lyon. Eventually he would become Father François Xavier Houang, priest of the Oratory. Much later I asked him why he had become a Christian and he said, in the first place, because of me, because of philosophy. This never struck me as bizarre: philosophy deals in absolutes and I have never said we could master them. Perhaps, as François thought, they master us. But that is not until much later, after the war. Not only a Christian and a priest, he also became a professor of Chinese philosophy at the École des Langues orientales and at the Sorbonne. He would lecture on Buddhism at the Institut catholique de Paris. He entered the Oratorian order, I believe, in 1952. For many years he was also vicar of Saint-Eustache near Les Halles in Paris. At François' invitation I once heard Olivier Messiaen perform "Apparitions de l'église éternelle" and several other remarkable pieces of music on its famous organ, the largest in the city. François was baptized in 1945, during the final months of the war.

I met him by chance, one spring, in a garden at the Université de Lyon. I believe it was 1936. It was spring, in any case. He was sitting on a wooden bench underneath a Japanese cherry tree in full bloom. I remember him, hunched over a large textbook in his lap. A few more inches and his forehead would have been resting on the page. At first I thought he was asleep. Fearing that he would fall and hit his head on the stones beneath the bench, I approached him and placed my hand on his shoulder. He nearly jumped out of his skin. Peering up at me he squinted and smiled before standing to his feet. The book fell from his lap. I sat down beside him. Picking up his book, he turned deferentially towards me.

"Young man," I asked, "what are you studying?"

"Sir, good morning [it was afternoon]. I study biology. I come from Shanghai. I am called François. And you, sir, how are you today?" He spoke woodenly but with careful accentuation. His intelligence was the first thing I noticed about him. At the same time I saw what anyone who meets him also first sees: his smile and his eyes. That day in the garden he had a mischievous grin and eyes of equal parts laughter and penetration. These were his most striking traits on our first encounter and they have never left him all the years I have known him.

"My name is Jean Wahl. I teach philosophy. I was born in Marseille, but grew up in Paris."

François' eyes squinted even more as he grinned. He reminded me faintly of the laughing Buddha. "And you are a philosopher, then?"

"Yes."

"Would you permit me to ask you a question?"

"Yes."

"What is, how do you say, the value of thought? I mean to say, what is the *use* of thinking, in this world, today?"

"Young man," I said, "There are many answers to that question. Before I attempt to give you one, tell me: why do you ask this strange question?"

"I can see the value of biology and the other sciences: they improve the material conditions of humanity. I can see the value of anything we endeavor to understand and to master because it alleviates suffering. But I do not see what philosophy does for human suffering except make it a problem and avoid concrete answers."

He spoke with a directness and penetration that was natural and only rarely can be taught.

"Yes," I responded, "the physical sciences, the technological sciences improve the material conditions of humanity. But what about the spiritual condition of humanity? Is there suffering present in our spirit?" I asked.

"I, well, yes, we must say that there is: desire is a suffering, longing is a suffering, despair, anger, sadness: all these are kinds of suffering . . ."

"Yes, they are: and ecstasy and pleasure are a suffering too. You look surprised. Pleasure is the state of enjoyment, of possessing something desired. There is no pleasure at all without an act of being-subject-to, of opening yourself to something else. To enjoy the feeling of the sun on my face I must subject myself to the light by moving out of the shade. That openness is a passivity; possessing the object of desire is first a being possessed by it, suffering it. If the desire or longing is extinguished, so is the pleasure or ecstasy of this possession. Pleasure includes within it the suffering of want. And the greatest pleasures reach the highest peaks of longing and wash in the ecstasy of identity between ache and joy, thirst and slaking, emptiness and being filled."

36

I paused, smiled, and gazed into the sky. Conversation was always one of my greatest sources of contentment. Sometimes the insights unfold from themselves and I become like a passive instrument, like an artist or musician through whom music flows.

"It is strange to think," I continued, "that both pleasure and pain are strangely, I mean 'weirdly' (as the Americans say), equal parts one another underneath, even though they are opposites, contradictories, the farthest from one another that you can get. Maybe like the body and spirit . . ."

François' eyes danced with wonder at the paradox. "And so, can we separate them at all, Professor? And if we can, should we separate them? It is my view — forgive me, monsieur, for speaking as if I have a right to a philosophical viewpoint — that in separating what is in essence intertwined, we unravel our humanity and find only useless abstraction. We must therefore always remain in the concrete, with what matters to us here and now, and this is the material conditions of human existence. Isn't this explanation enough for us to pave over them for the betterment of the world?"

"Abstracting from the Marxist undercurrent of your thinking, this is my view precisely, young man. And I will also say that we can and must distinguish these most basic dimensions of ourselves, body and soul — just as we can distinguish pleasure and pain, or joy and suffering (if we do not we are probably suffering from a serious psychological malady, a madness!) — but we cannot and must not divide them. For if you enter into the depths or roots of one, you always find the other. And this is because at the living root of our body is feeling, affectivity, which is charged with energy, the raw energy at the base of our intelligence. So, now, with that said, I think we have reached your question."

"So what is the use of philosophy — a purely 'spiritual' kind of reflection? . . . Excuse me: I am sorry, I am not speaking clearly. But do you know what I try to say?"

"I certainly do. And I will only give you one answer of the many that are possible, an ancient one: *thinking of this sort has no use.* This answer is venerable and a good starting place. Philosophy, at its apex, when it is thinking about the highest things, is use-less: it does not make anything or choose any course of action. It sets itself apart from the questions of living and surviving. It sets aside the entire world of experience and thinks about its meaning. It seeks one thing: knowledge of what is, explanations of the principles of things. But this use-less-ness gives it its supreme value."

"And what is that?"

"It is the only means to happiness."

"But can it bring about the end of sorrow, of suffering, of sickness, and pain?"

"No. But these are excluded from it itself *when* it is engaged in thinking about the highest things. It gives a beatitude, a blessedness, a joy beyond that of power or control or possession. And from within that beatitude, the entire world of our embodied existence and its exigencies is perhaps transfigured in its light as only shadowy extensions of this one act of knowing . . ."

"The 'principles of things'?"

"Yes: 'first principles'— those things, or maybe that one thing, that one reality beyond this and that and which is the reason why all this and that that is is what it is."

The young man repeated my words carefully: " . . . the reason why all this and that that is is what it is . . ." He smiled: "What is that reason . . . reason itself?"

"Some have said that. And they have also said at the same time, God: divinity. Pure intelligence bounded only by its perfect identity with itself in the sheer bliss of knowledge that is pure action with nothing else remaining. Contemplation contemplating itself. Around which the world and all that is in it turns, all held in place by an affiliation, an attraction, a desire, a being drawn toward this divine bliss simply by virtue of being."

François looked at me with rapt attention.

"Of course," I continued, "I am only speaking in the train of one philosopher: Aristotle. With this vision he has been singularly influential on Western thought."

"God . . ." said François contemplatively. "God . . ."

"And yourself," I said. "Whatever you are, you are a being who can utter that word, who can ask that question. The absolute question. The question that, as far as the history of philosophy is concerned, is at the basis of every question we can ask."

He straightened and turned to me. There was anxiety and ambition in his voice: "Tell me, Professor: God: is God *personal?*" He took a deep breath: "I mean, can God be known? Or rather: is God alive?"

"I do not know. Just as I do not know if you and I persist in some way after death. I do not *know* where we come from or where we are going. Philosophy cannot answer these questions with the certainty of . . ."

He frowned: "Then philosophy's uselessness is even more useless. The happiness it proposes in its contemplation of the Absolute is short-lived!" His frown was tinged with disgust and evinced a stormy retreat into his youthful Marxism. I responded:

"Philosophy cannot answer these questions, but it can and does ask them. And asking them, deepening them, immersing in their wonderful meaningfulness and ever-greater demand to the point of a kind of supreme decision, of a leap into your own humanity — that is where philosophy takes you."

My new Chinese student paused. His expression changed. He took a deep breath:

"I see. Thinking takes you very far. It is essential." He paused again and stated, resolutely: "I want to study philosophy."

He stood up, shook my hand vigorously, and walked away. That was it! That conversation under the white blooms of a Japanese cherry — I am surprised that there is nothing that I have lost from it, and I have repeated to you every word as if here and now it was just happening before us — it persuaded him to give up his course in biology. The very next week he was sitting in the front row of my class.

François, in fact, spent the rest of his life investigating what he called "the metaphysical foundations of personal existence" in Western and Eastern philosophies. He saw personal existence as the summit of reality from which we humans are privileged to stand and peer out onto the vast differentiated terrains of being. But his question was: what is the basis or source of this summit? Is our *personal* existence, joining freedom and understanding, simply the unthinkable or perhaps barely thinkable point of access to summits upon summits above us? For him, religion, with its personal and free divinity, its God who is both unbounded sea of reality and singularizing voice of address, both terrifying holiness and all-encompassing love, draws philosophy ineluctably into itself where what is lived, through prayer, through ritual action, through reflection and its higher modes of meditation, is precisely the very access to those summits beyond the dark, teeming clouds circling densely above our tiny human aerie . . .

— What about yourself?

I think I heard your voice . . . The very air around us vibrates with unseen life. And the chiaroscuro of light deepens all around. (Are you asking me that question?) I . . . I certainly pose it to myself. And with what force it assails me! How afraid and giddy I am, as if struck by lightning! The paradox, the problem is that one cannot avoid this most unphilosophical question without failing philosophy, without failing the perpetual experiment of humanity, new with every cry of the newborn child! What about that, my dear, mysterious stranger? I share this with you alone. It is our secret. It is one of my deepest secrets. It is the secret of all of us. François Houang, a Chinese student in beginner's wooden French: he forced it on me with his devilish grin. He forces it on me even now.

He unveiled it to me in the garden in Lyon! He lifted the sheet, the burlap sack of concerns, and of fears, and of difficulties — those difficulties . . . that religious people call "sins," failures, wounds peppering my soul. Wounds that never heal. Do they ever heal?

How difficult it is for me to look this in the face! And when I begin to — here I am: it is your gaze that I meet! How difficult the wounds make this essential act! To do so would mean to look at myself as I really am. But here I am: "What about yourself": your words, they gaze into, they pierce my being! I can barely raise my eyes.

Every support is falling away! I cannot stand, I cannot now face what faces me. To do that is to see, or rather to see myself being seen by — by what? — the Almighty, the Personal God of religion, whose freedom terrifies me! Can I risk annihilation? Well, can I?

But here I am. You alone, an eternally newborn child from

regions far beyond the sheltering world on the other side of the gate behind me . . . Can you tell me the answer? I am old. But: how young I am when this question rears on its hind legs within me!

I am asking you — now in this moment, it is clear — because this is the one question that has always driven me — no: it guides me. It burns me. It has driven me from here to there and back again, across seas and up the winding mountain trail where I first began to speak to you, where I first began telling you this story. Now I have woken here — or am I dreaming? — on the borderlands of some interstitial worlds. This question: it has held me in its iron grip. It has threatened me, and it has sustained me at one and the same time. That is how it burns. I can only close my eyes to it. I can only distance myself from it. I do this without even trying: to climb the rocks, to risk the danger, is the only way to keep from falling into the abyss. But at what cost?!

The cost is everything. I may fall anyway: that is out of my hands!

I risk myself. But I am and only am a risk. That is all I am as a personal being, an existing being. But — I still myself: I am alienated from religion. (How honest I am at this moment: it startles me . . .) Why? It is not just I. Religion is, if it is anything at all, the path of access to God as God is, in his transcendence and freedom. But God is everywhere, and he is himself one and the same in every time and place. In every thing.

God transcends religion. Religion also veils God, obscures him. It even wants to strangle God until he is dead. Religion at its mystical heights itself teaches me this. I am a man of the margins. And I will remain on these margins. I will remain at a distance from religion, as a testimony against religion and as a testimony for God. And as a testimony, then, for religion as well. A testimony for the Reality at its base, which suffuses it and which has always spilled out beyond it.

The Reality it can never reach but yet has already reached by its very being what it is.

It is that Reality, the unthinkable God to whom my being only ever testifies: in his excessive absence I acknowledge the radical presence to which that absence, that distance, testifies; in his presence I acknowledge the absence to which that presence testifies. When it is dark I long for the light; when it is light I long for the dark. When the quiet, shy whisper within me ventures to squeak an oh so tremulous "I believe," another voice rages through it to say, "but . . . BUT, I *do not believe!*" And when the raging voice feels self-sufficient, proud, all-encompassing, then I see through its posturing, its massive affectation of power. And behind it, even within it, at its source, I feel the question, the enigma, the strange certitude that does not go away but is itself the cool, unfathomable depths of the turbulent, smashing surface of the consciousness of my being.

And I *am* both voices. Light and Dark. When both are one, *as they really are*, then I will stand in the middle, at one with myself. As for now — even now — I can only be a man of the borderlands, inhabiting the alienated edge, crossing, always crossing the expanse and climbing, always climbing the rock. I therefore retain my perch on the little summit of human existence. But I see the mountain face soaring above and the sea roiling far below.

If there are messengers from worlds beyond the ranges of humanity's roving then to me, maybe they are a little like François Houang . . .

— And why, might not there be?

I again hear your voice in my head. I drown in the open torrent of your face. If science . . . How strange are my words to me; they are so far away, and tremble like a dry leaf threatened by the least puff of breath . . . Breath. (The sea is breathing . . .) If science "has no need of that hypothesis" to proceed into the quantitative infinities proper to it, that relative damming does not keep the existence of transcendent, qualitatively other worlds on worlds from flooding all around it. I speak as a fool: but, I am only speaking as a human, and still lingering at the gates — Are you laughing at me? I see that you are. No matter. There is more knowledge in your face than in all the wisdom on the mountain or in the seas. This makes me content. For your face, come from so far away, and yet (how?) it has been always so near; your face, it is kind but it is fire . . .

The angels. Unfathomable intelligences inhabiting unknown depths and ranges beyond the fractured crust of existence that is our world. And how are such beings, the angels, maybe a little like my little Chinese Francis? There are two reasons: (1) Angels are greater than us, but — at least as much as we know (know? Ha!) about them, which is only relative, and a tiny fragment as pertains to their ontological magnitude — they serve us and our world (or they seek to destroy it: but I once made a vow, which I would like to keep, that I am not getting into any demonology). (2) Angels are one part beautiful and one part terrible: and in them these two traits are not contradictory. But you will understand this — I mean about François Houang — as my story unfolds.

After thinking these thoughts, or some of them — I think them now as if new; but they signify, they are bonded with memory of the past — the past is memory and yet, somehow, so is the future . . . and the present bleeds into both — I am being stretched — agony and ecstasy — how much time lies within this moment of time? Infinite dimensions are contained in the potency of a single point — nothing in itself and yet containing everything possible — I confess I am confused, here, about time and space — Or do I see? — The course of things in my memory, here, seems more than a one way street — I opened the letter from François, sitting by the fire or within it in my hotel apartment on Rue des Beaux Arts, a one-day's free man. Now I will tell you what it said.

8 | FRANÇOIS' LETTER

Christmas Eve 1941

Monsieur le Professeur Jean Wahl.
From his student and disciple François Houang Kia-tcheng.

My Dear Master. I read a passage from Descartes just yesterday. He says that "those who move only very slowly may make much greater progress if they always follow the right path than those who run but stray from it."[*] Descartes is speaking of virtue and vice. You know this passage well, I am certain. The "right path" he is speaking of is the human path itself, and one may proceed along it poorly, unraveling into vice, or proceed well (and more slowly, laboriously), developing in virtue. Descartes also observes here that "the greatest souls are just as capable of the greatest vices as of the greatest virtues." In my humble and small estimation, Monsieur, you are a great soul and I wonder where you are, or rather, how you are along this human path that we are condemned to walk and to crawl. Your situation compels me to add to Descartes' reflection: the greatest situations, that is, the most acute ones, the most intense, whether good or bad, joyful or disastrous, are sites where the possibilities for greatness or badness — well, let me just say it — for

---

[*] This quotation comes from Descartes' *Discourse on Method*. I use the English translation of Desmond Clark (NY: Penguin, 2003), 6. — W. C. H.

46

good or evil are comparably magnified. Maybe you see, maybe you are now seeing what is at stake in the world a little more clearly, or better, more deeply, profoundly, if also with the same difficult vagueness that perplexes us all and seems to be a permanent feature of our present existence. I do know this: that in thinking of you this is what I am led to contemplate. But who am I to write these words to you? I am in Lyon. I am free. This is what I think about when I think about you: and the merit of words does not always restrict itself to the merit of the one saying them.

As I write, in fact, I am sitting on the bench in the garden where we first met. I come here, every day if possible, as a sort of simple act of solidarity with you, as an act of memory. You are in prison unjustly. I can only imagine the sufferings you are presently enduring. It horrifies me to imagine you there, but I do not hesitate to enter into this horror of ignorance for it motivates me to do two things: to pray and to act.

To pray: I do not hesitate to say such an uncomfortable or awkward thing in this letter, and not because I only barely hold myself back from the despair that you will never read these words, but because now, in these circumstances, this seems right and necessary and urgent. You did not know this, but I have had a kind of awakening here in Lyon. I have found something: there are eyes buried deep inside of us that sleep. And they can be awoken, just like ears and hands and noses and tongues that, once enlivened from their deep slumber within us in the cave of this world, can sense that other world which is there, everywhere, on the other side of our body's senses and of their world. We possess within us organs that correspond to another place, a higher world. Here in this world of trials and errors we are tied down: we cannot reach that world, we can only brush against it, see it out of the corner of our eyes, hear its vague rumors, taste it, and touch it, however, through the joys and longings and sorrows of our experience here. And yet: we do not have to leave this world to find it, though we must *eclipse* this world. But this is done only through burrowing ever more deeply into the present moment, *the here and now*, until its contradictions give way to spiritual vistas that cannot be expressed but only experienced, undergone. One must press into the contradictions until they shatter. And there is no guarantee . . . I am now thinking — that is, with these last words — a little like you, a little as you have taught me to think, and I hope this interpretation of your thinking, though distinctive and existentially unique and as different as we are from one another, rings true with the recognition of a human authenticity that you have always taught me to look for and to find, and, when found, to grapple with until I am formed by it. I am writing wildly and strangely. But there is every reason for this. I have so much to speak with you about and to ask you about.

I said a moment ago that my horror and ignorance motivates me to act. There is no choice but the decision to act. I am grateful beyond words that you have taught me this. And I am, in fact, acting on your behalf. I have brought your situation before some of the Casuists of Lyon whose concern for you matches my own. Father Henri de Lubac in particular mentions you frequently and with affection. There are some here who started a journal, *Témoignage chrétien*, which is completely underground and doing much good in reminding people that the oil of Nazi ideology does not mix with Christian and French water and in fact makes it worthless to drink. I even saw a letter from Abbé Monchanin. He remains in India, immersing himself in that intellectual Ganges that finds such profound and unspeakable correspondences with the stream of Western thought. Father de Lubac showed his letter to me when I visited him and brought up your name. The Abbé mentions again his debt to you, of your reading of Plato's *Parmenides*, which he places within a Neoplatonic framework to signify that fundamental drive to a higher unity beyond, or rather through, the play of the one and the many, of unity and differentiation that forms the intelligible horizon of our existence. This interpretation of your thinking is a key to the Abbé's own thought and a principle of his constructive encounter with the spiritual monism of India's great intellectual masters. And perhaps also with my patrimonial civilization. But that is another day's conversation, in another garden, under another blossoming tree.

I hope this brings you comfort in your trial. There are many who owe so much to you, and, in fact, who love you. I am only one among them. But, my Dear Master, there is more to my action than private solidarity and kindling indignation at your situation. If you are reading this letter, in fact, it means that my actions have not been in vain. I cannot say more now than what you already know: there is an appointment waiting for you at an American university. Your brother — how kind he continues to be to me — says that you are aware of this. The trouble *was* how to get you out of the camp. I write this in hope that you will read this letter and therefore I state this in the past tense. And that was the whole trouble, was it not?! But even now, if we succeeded in climbing that impossible mountain, there is more to be done: a sea must be crossed.

If you are reading this letter, if my actions have not been in vain, the trouble is now: how to get you out of Paris. I need confirmation of your situation, that you are free, that you are in hiding, that you are able to flee, when the time comes. Coordinating this we — I mean your brother and I from Lyon, you yourself of course, and I hope, a few friends among the resistance in Paris — can work out a feasible plan. I have been assured that the Casuists in Lyon can help us push this plan forward. Please write.

Your devoted servant,

F. H.

I never received his other letters. They must have been intercepted at La Santé and, if he sent them there after my transfer to Drancy, they were incinerated. I was intrigued, and maybe a little startled, to see François become close to the Christian intellectuals in Lyon. They are, of course, many, and they are brilliant, and many of them good friends and colleagues, even inspirations (I am thinking primarily of Abbé Jules Monchanin, whom he mentioned). I thought, even then, that I could see the outlines of a religious conversion in this letter, and, as I mentioned before, this turned out to be correct. But what first struck me so powerfully within it was the name of Monchanin, which danced off the page as if charged with electricity. That name was like a living presence, noticed in the shadows along the peripheries of my mind but seldom directly perceived. To me and to many others that man possessed a sort of saintliness (natural or supernatural it does not matter, and that distinction, with him, and with the world's saintly persons, only seems to obscure the essential) that gave his actions and words a gravity or weight that the rest of us do not have, but which can only be recognized in them through our memory. In the presence of one of these saintly persons you are always tempted to overlook them. It is so peculiar and remarkable. And then I recalled something with a shudder — I am shuddering now: forgive me: how the words shake in my head as I speak! I recalled the terrible dream I had while sick within the Gates of Drancy: the sewer, the sea, the monster, the mountain hurtling across the expanse and the ascetic wise man descending its face to gaze into my naked soul transfixed against the grate. I do not remember if this figure literally had the face of the Abbé Monchanin in my dream. But I do know that that figure and the Abbé are, since that moment when my eyes crossed his name in François' letter, tied together in my mind. It seemed to me then and it seems to me now that the virtue and serene beauty that the Abbé himself possesses so intimately were manifest in that dream with an individuated purity and substantiality. I will never grasp the significance of any of this, but I cannot shake the strangeness of it all. As if, at death, you would give me a key to open the mystery of all the scattered fragments of my entire existence, then that dream, that world-defining dream, that dream to the side of death's door, within the prison walls, it too would be comprehended as well. Maybe that dream is itself the lock which that key would turn. Maybe Abbé Monchanin is himself the keyhole . . .

— *Maybe it is you* . . .

I am raving again. But the fact is that sometimes you feel like there are people you encounter who are more human because also they are other or more than that. I met two like this in Lyon: Abbé Monchanin and François Houang. Children also have this quality. I can only think there are traces of this — whatever it is — in all of us. It is something close to the center of who we are, even if it is buried under much wreckage.

The "Casuists in Lyon" in his penultimate line was of course a reference to the Jesuits previously mentioned in his letter. I enjoyed Pascal's *Provincial Letters* as much as anyone, but, like it or not, the Jesuits of France were playing a fervent part among the various organizations and quasi-organizations of French resistance against the Nazis. It was them, it seemed, that I would have to contact in Paris. But did I need to? Could I not stay here, hidden in my hotel apartment with my books, with Gilles Alain and with Monsieur and Madame David? Why even risk the flight to Lyon when it is not clearly necessary? Yet again my feet longed to drive roots into my home, into the city of my love. And yet again it was only the pressure of external forces threatening my life joined to the pleading of friends that broke through my natural inertia and caused me to act. These external forces, both for and against me, were moving, ordering themselves, gathering without my awareness, as I convalesced with Gilles Alain. And like a squall that descends on a man in a rudderless boat on the edge of the sea, dragging him where it will, so comes the violent reprisal of Theodor Dannecker, the Nazi captain who since my arrest made my terror a personal obsession and under whose nose I was delivered from the camp.

9 | A WORD FROM THE CAMP

The life of Gilles Alain, wracked by the conditions of the camp and tortured by the disease, hung in the balance for days. On reaching my apartment at Rue des Beaux Arts, he was dangerously dehydrated: his insides, as he put it, smiling, were "as dry as a grandmother's *corsage.*" He kept his humor to the end. He had also contracted pneumonia during our winter day's walk from Drancy to the center of Paris. Only the attention of Madame David saved him. And she restored him to a modicum of health. In fact, she restored both of us, giving us the strength to face what was to come. It came quickly.

Madame David, as I said, was the best of France. She brought three large and hearty meals a day to us as we convalesced. In fact, I spent the first four days of my freedom without leaving the apartment. Those first days we felt safe and maybe even a little hopeful. But there, in that world (as in any world I can comprehend), there is only one constant: change.

On the fifth day the sun appeared in a cloudless sky.

I had moved my psychoanalyst's couch before the window and was bathing, as well as I could, in the cool warmth of winter light. Madame David entered. With her walked a young woman, a girl. I knew her, or at least I knew that I know her: I had seen her before, but in another place, another world . . . Together they crossed the room and stood before me. The girl was wearing a green pea coat. She looked like she was on her way to school. Madame David said: "This is Alice Beauchamp. She has a message for you. I thought to bring her up here immediately. It is urgent. She is only to place it directly into your hands. She is on strict orders from . . ." Her face turned dark and she interjected: "Did I do the right thing? I hope I am right to bring her to you . . ."

Before I could answer, the girl spoke. Her name, her face, her beautiful, innocent face . . .

"Monsieur, I am pleased to see you are recovering. L'infirmière générale, Mademoiselle Monod, has given me this. It is indeed urgent."

Blood dropped from my face. A feeling of anxiety and nausea began to turn in my stomach. My chest tightened. I recognized her.

"Alice, my girl . . . Drancy, I . . ." With some effort I pulled myself partway up on the couch and waved my hand vaguely. "Her name, the head nurse I mean, her name is Monod? I never knew her name. She saved my health. I remember you. You are kind, child." I reached out my trembling hand. She took it.

"You have Mademoiselle Monod to thank for your escape. She placed your name on the list at the very last minute. You see . . . you could not know this but you were not on the list of the sick to be released. In fact, you were, but then the list . . . the German Officer, Dannecker, he struck your name from it when he reviewed it for final approval. L'infirmière générale, she risked much . . . she had your name placed back on the list. She pleaded ignorance: a mix-up of lists, a bureaucratic mistake. There is no one to blame. Several copies of the list, several revisions were in fact circulated . . . This was our opportunity."

A shadow passed over her face. She continued: "Dannecker . . . the camp superintendent . . . he, that man has returned. And he is, in fact, enraged. He came for you . . . to interrogate you. When he learned that you had escaped he strangled a man. I screamed. It was just a man, a prisoner, standing there in the nurse's station." She looked up. "He wrenched that man's neck with such cold brut . . ."

Her voice trailed off. She did not cry but her face brought back shadows of the fear and sadness that it wore earlier that day.

"How did you find me here?" I whispered, struggling not to be overcome with the emotions crashing into one another on the swelling surface of the sea within my chest. I was alive. That man was strangled in my place. She collected herself and continued:

"Mademoiselle Monod: she is *une résistante*, I would say, *une résistante notoire*. Did you not know this?" Alice paused and continued: "She has been in contact with a woman, Alice Carbanne, here in Paris, a socialist, a *résistante* as well, in fact a figure in *Libération Nord* . . ." Her voice turned to a whisper. Madame David began to weep.

Alice continued, "Madame Carbanne contacted Mademoiselle Monod about your situation. There was no hope. And then there was."

I gasped at the name of Alice Carbanne. This name, these two words were the only ones in all that she said on which I could grasp. The rest of what she said was like a rock face, on which I was slipping . . .

"There is also a man, a Chinese man in Lyon. With your brother and some other persons, religious persons, Jesuits in fact . . . they are all mobilizing for you. Anyway, there is no time to lose. There is a message here from Mademoiselle Monod. And I carry, in my mind, the remaining instructions. Here."

55

She pulled from her breast pocket a tiny square of paper, folded in half. Our eyes traced its solemn path in the air as if it were drawn from a reliquary. She placed it in my hands. I opened it. The message was simple. It said:

Sir
Your enemy has returned
He has named you "Public Enemy. To be shot on sight."
He is searching for you. You are not safe
You must leave
Follow the instructions
Farewell.

And lower on the page:

There are friends near and far who are helping you

As I was reading this message, as I was reeling from the venom of Dannecker, his words, quoted in the letter, inciting invisible wounds within me, wounds that he inflicted on me in prison and in the camp, Gilles Alain entered from the bedroom, wrapped in a blanket the way we wore them about Drancy — covering our heads, hands tightly grasping them under our chins. He sat down on the settee in the middle of the room and gazed out the window. I looked up at Alice's face. The other Alice was in my mind, Alice Carbanne: she was in fact a long-time friend, a family friend. I forget when we first met. My head was swimming, but my body was electrified with excitement. The little Alice spoke:

"I am to tell you. Are you ready? You seem . . . Monsieur Wahl? Madame David, can we get him some water, please?"

She sat down on the edge of my couch. Her slender hands were cradled together in her lap. She spoke calmly. This comforted me. I longed to place my hands within hers.

"I am to tell you, Monsieur Wahl, that you are to make contact immediately with Alice Carbanne. She and the others in Paris will organize your escape to the *zone libre*.

"I will go to Mâcon and stay with my family," I said absently. I sat up and said urgently: "Gilles Alain. He will come with me." I paused, trying to gather myself, and then: "Alice Carbanne, I know her, I know her apartment, not far from my father's house . . ."

Gilles Alain stood, wobbled, and sat back down. "I am getting better, but to flee again . . ."

"He needs a few more days!" said Madame David with a hoarse cry. She hurried to his side and sat down beside him, grabbing his hand.

Alice stood: "I must return to Drancy." She looked at Gilles Alain and back to me: "He must go, too, or you must part. They will kill him if he is with you . . ."

I looked at Gilles Alain: "You cannot stay in this city. The time is now. We must leave."

Gilles Alain muttered helplessly. Then he looked to the window and whispered: "Okay, I will come."

Alice hid her thumbs behind the lapels of her coat: "Be careful, Monsieur Wahl, and God be with you."

Madame David stood and accompanied Alice to the door. They left together, Madame David looking back at us as she closed the door. Gilles Alain and I quickly made a concrete plan of action. I was to go, immediately, to Alice Carbanne's apartment. Gilles Alain was to make preparations for departure, and to be ready, at a moment's notice, to flee. At this he only wandered around the room with an absent look on his face. All that was there was mine. Even the clothes on his back were not his but were provided by Madame David. I told him to ask Madame David for a few suitcases. There were two of my own under the bed. I would return shortly, hopefully with more information, and then we would decide what to take with us on our flight from Paris. From the Nazi, Theodor Dannecker.

10 | A CLOSE CALL

I walked down Rue Bonaparte to the river and turned left on Quai Voltaire. I could not bring myself to descend into the metro. To be under the earth: it scared me. I would cross the Seine at Pont d'Iena under the shadow of the Tour Eiffel at the Champ de Mars. Crossing the southeast corner of the Jardins du Trocadero, I would walk up Rue de Passy until I reached her apartment, just a few blocks northeast from my parents' place on Avenue Colonel-Bonnet.

As I reached the Tour Eiffel, I recalled my walk, with a few of my students, those several months ago toward the Bois de Bologne and Avenue Foch in response to Dannecker's summons to the Nazi headquarters. I thought of my colleague at the *Nouvelle Revue Française*, Pierre Drieu La Rochelle, for the first time since we spoke on the phone that day, when by his voice I knew he betrayed me to advance his career. That son of a bitch! I hate him, but less now than before. It is my pity for him that grows. Avenue Foch was in the same *arrondissement* as my parents' address, only a few kilometers north, in fact. This disturbed me. I thought of Theodore Dannecker in his office at Avenue Foch, interrogating and arresting other Jewish persons of interest; I thought of his brown leather gloves, blue veins pulsing in his neck, his coldness, his calculated madness. Even so I decided to loop by my parents' apartment before reaching Alice Carbanne. This was an impulse. I would not have done this if I knew what was to happen next.

59

I turned left at Place du Costa Rica and walked down Rue Raynouard until I reached Avenue du Colonel-Bonnet on my right. I gazed down the street. My parents' building was about a quarter of the way down, on the right, number 40. Cars were parked along the entire left-hand side of the street — except one — a black Traction Avant, sitting directly in front of their building, a steady stream of grey exhaust dissolving behind it in the cold air. I could have mistaken it for my father's car, if I had not abandoned it in the alley behind the *Orient d'Or* in Saint-Quentin, to the north, so many months ago when I first fled Paris before the German invasion. Standing there at the end of the street I thought I could see the statue of a man sitting in the back seat, wearing a hat. Perhaps it was, I thought with a shudder, an officer's visor cap, an officer whom I know quite well . . .

And perhaps it was him. As I stood there, in the middle of the street, the front door of the apartment building opened, and two German soldiers walked out and stepped into the car which promptly drove away. I stared at the taillights of the car as they flashed and turned right, disappearing onto Rue Alfred Bruneau.

The Germans had just visited my father's apartment.

Hesitating for a moment, I decided to stop by my old address, where I lived with my father and stepmother for several years until the birds croaking day and night in Passy — I mean my stepmother, but not only her — forced me to find quiet, which I found at the hotel on Rue des Beaux Arts. I walked up the street, advancing quickly, heart beating wildly in the hollow of my chest.

Entering the building I ascended the familiar stairs to the first floor. Number 3, at the end of the hall. Resolute, I knocked on the door. Before I could drop my arm, Agathe, the young woman renting the apartment from my parents, answered. She cracked open the door. I could see her shaking. She stood as if lost, her childlike face staring out at me from across an abyss. I pushed her, a little roughly, into the apartment and shut the door.

She took a few awkward steps backwards and trembled. "A German patrol was just here . . . Are they there, on the stairs? Did they see you?" Her speech was confused. We sat down. "They were looking for you!" she said excitedly, glancing at the door. She drew the back of her hand to her forehead in a dramatic gesture and fell back into her seat. In another context, perhaps, one could have very nearly mistaken her for an American actress. She grabbed a pillow, drew it to her chest, and returned it to its place on the couch. I told her that I saw the Germans drive away. "In the street . . . I, I came to ask you," I continued, "what they said . . . and . . . what you said."

She stopped trembling and a fierce look flashed across her face. "I told them I had not seen you. One of them searched the apartment while the other asked me questions."

"What did he ask you?"

"He asked me if you were here. I said no. He asked me if I had seen you. 'No.' If I knew where you might be. I said I heard you were in prison at La Santé. (Actually, I knew you were at Drancy. I have spoken with your father several times by phone.) He told me you had escaped and that you were likely still in Paris. That you might contact me. I asked what you had done. He told me you were an 'enemy of the state,' a dangerous man. Then he asked me if I knew you were a Jew. I said 'Yes, but what does that have to do with me?' The two men stared at me for a moment and they thanked me for my cooperation. They left. That was it."

"Did you tell them about where I had been living, my hotel, in the sixth?"

"No, I did not know where you were living. Only that you did not live here with your father and mother anymore, for several years. That you had moved away. I told them I did not know where. That I had no contact with you, only with your father. But they are safe, very safe, in the south . . ."

"But you told them that I did not live here before my arrest?!"

"Yes."

"Oh my God."

"I told them this. Why does it . . . I thought it would demonstrate how little I know . . . Oh my God, I did, I did not think . . ." She cradled her forehead in her hands and stared at the floor.

"He will make inquiries. He will find me. He is crazed. I am what he hates . . ." I was nearly shouting.

"Who, *Professeur*, who hates you?" She screamed back at me in a hoarse, cracked voice.

"Agathe," I said quietly, looking into her eyes, "I must go now. Thank you for protecting me. If they return, call me at . . ."

"No! No, Monsieur Wahl," she said, standing. "Do not tell me where you hide. I do not think I should know. My ignorance is your best protection, no? No?!," she asked again.

She looked at me with innocent impatience. I stood. Her eyes were beautiful, and they sought consolation.

"Yes, there is nothing else you can do. You are right. I must go."

She grabbed my hands and held them tightly. Her eyes were closed. I gave her no comfort and received none from her. Neither of us spoke.

I left.

11 | MESSAGE IN A BOTTLE

Outside of the door to my father's apartment I half expected to find Dannecker's men waiting. Descending, I felt the same fear as the bottom of the stairway came into view, and again at the front door of the building. No one was there: the hallway, the stairs, the front entry of the building, all desolate. I peeked through the glass doors and rushed into the street. No car, no soldiers. I turned right and walked through the few streets to Alice Carbanne's apartment. I stumbled twice. My feet were numb. The wind was cold, but I was sweating under my hat. I entered the building's front door, which was propped open.

An old man was washing the stone floor of the long entryway with a mop. He gave me an absent wave, incongruent and cheerful, and returned to his work. The internal door was also open so I did not ring her apartment from below but ascended the stairs.

I rasped at her door and waited. No movement inside. I could hear muffled voices and a chair scraping the floor behind another door a few steps away. I knocked again, quietly. She was not home. I took a scrap of paper out of the internal pocket of my jacket. It had been there for so long . . . It looked as if it had been wetted and dried several times. On it were the details of books by some English philosophers I once studied. I wrote a large J. in heavy script above the book information on the front side and, in similar script, a .W at the top of the backside, positioning it just to the left of where the J. was placed. If she held up the paper to light, the .W would faintly show through the paper as W. and thus, on the front, she would see my initials, J. W.

Below the .W on the back of the paper I scribbled: "L'Hotel, Rue des Beaux Arts" and slipped it under her door. I was afraid to leave any other details. I imagined that she would piece together the clues with little trouble. I could not remember if she knew of my occupancy at this address or if she, too, thought I still lived with my father. . . Anyway, it was of course a famous hotel and perhaps there were lots of reasons why it would be scribbled on a scrap of paper. This precaution, though, seemed right: she was, as my little messenger had said, a *résistante*, a member of Libération Nord, and one like that could not be too careful. What would a Nazi do with a piece of scrap bibliographical paper on her floor? If she were somehow caught and interrogated it is not a given that they would associate her and her work with my fugitive self.

Descending the stairs of Alice Carbanne's building I suddenly felt how taxing this day's *escapade* had been. I took the metro back to my hotel. Under the ground I grew sick.

I began also to grow afraid.

12 | CONTACT

S everal days, perhaps a week passed. Nothing happened. Gilles Alain grew stronger every day. We played cards. We listened to music. We spoke of the future. Together we packed four large suitcases with my books and papers. Madame David had my suitcases shipped to Paul's address in Mâcon. This would, I thought, serve as a clear communication to him that I was on the move. I dared not try to send him a letter. Two further suitcases and a small trunk were filled with everything else: some clothes, personal articles, and the books I could hot bear to place in the mail system. And then we waited.

Two days later, in the afternoon, Madame David burst into my apartment. Unable to catch her breath, she panted for several moments and then said: "Monsieur: there is a phone call for you at the desk downstairs. You can take it in the lobby or in the bar."

I rushed down the stairs and entered the restaurant. Ordering a drink, I sat at the far end of the bar. The bartender placed the bar's black rotary telephone before me and walked away. I picked up the receiver and waited. No one was there. I cleared my throat. A voice on the line began to speak.

"Monsieur Wahl. Hello."

"Hello."

"This is Monsieur Wahl with whom I am speaking?"

"Yes, who is this?"

"I am a friend."

"A friend of whom?"

Silence.

"I am a friend of your friends," said the voice finally.

"My brother?"

"Among others."

"Who?"

"I do not want to say. I would like to meet with you. Soon."

"Okay. What is this about?"

"I will tell you when we meet."

"When should we meet?"

"Meet me in an hour, in front of Rothschild Frères Banque at Place de l'Opera."

I sat at the bar staring at my drink. "Was this some kind of trap? Did Dannecker so quickly discover my location?" Dannecker. Fear always brings him to mind, even now, after so many years... "But if he did know where I was," I continued thinking, "then why would he not come here to arrest me?" Based on this reasoning I decided to go meet this nameless voice at l'Opera. It was the next, necessary move on the chessboard. I could not do nothing. I finished my drink and walked out the door. Crossing the Seine at Pont des Arts I walked west along the river to the metro station at Pont Neuf, just above the eastern tip of the Île de la Cité.

The bell towers of Notre-Dame de Paris were silent. I see them in my mind as I recall this moment. Rising above the frozen stream of white-grey buildings, the cathedral's sharp central spire set against the background of dark clouds: this was the last thing I saw as I descended into the ground.

Climbing the metro steps at Place de l'Opera, my heart began to race. I crossed over Avenue de l'Opera on the Eastern side and leaned against a building to catch my breath. I lit a cigarette, which calmed me. The building was on the Western side of the Place, but for some reason or none I decided to approach it by walking along the street around its entire perimeter. I approached the bank from the Opera House and stood on its front steps. The sidewalk was nearly as busy as the street. I did not wait long. A man approached me. He was short, with a thick black moustache and nervous eyes. He carried a slender briefcase of black leather and wore a large black overcoat. The coat was unbuttoned as if he had either been walking a long distance or had just descended out of one of the buildings ringing the wide circle of road. The chain of a silver pocket watch was hanging from his waistcoat like an officer's decoration. I could not decide if he was a lawyer or minor government official.

"Good day," he said, smiling stiffly. "Let us go to Le Grand Café Capucines. We can talk there; it is large, very busy."

As we walked together around the perimeter of Place de l'Opera, he told me in precise terms the details of "your plan": I was to board tomorrow's 4 a.m. train at Gare de Lyon and disembark at a certain town. The train would arrive there at three in the afternoon. "Once you are there," he continued, "you are to forget the name of the town." I was to wait on the station platform until a man with an automobile came for me. He would give me further instructions. The man repeated these details twice. I do not recall that we spoke of anything else, for not long after he finished speaking we reached the front door of the café. Here he turned to me and said: "Now, that is all I have to tell you. I am going here. You may go where you wish."

Taking my leave, I returned to the metro station in the center of Place de l'Opera and returned home. A heavy wet snow began to fall. Crossing back over Pont des Arts, the growing suspicion that I had forgotten something finally broke over me: Gilles Alain! I failed to mention that he was to come with me! "Well, a car can carry two passengers just as well as one," I decided. When I emerged from the metro, the sky was dark. The streetlamps were not illuminated.

13 | THE FACE

I slept in my clothes. At least I wore them to bed: I did not sleep. This was the first night in fact since our escape three weeks before that I had trouble sleeping. Compared to straw scratched about over stone floor, the psychoanalyst's couch made for a very pleasant night. But that night, the night of our flight, I could not settle down. It was as if the terror and apprehension that haunted me in the camp at night had finally caught me outside the gates. As soon as I turned out the light I was seized with a strong disquiet.

At precisely three in the morning Louis-Baptiste knocked and entered. "The woman," he said, referring to Madame David, "will stay in our rooms. She bids you both a fond farewell."

Louis-Baptiste had arranged a car to take us to Gare de Lyon. It was already waiting in the alley behind the hotel. I opened the bedroom door to rouse Gilles Alain but decided to wait. First, we would take down the luggage, then I would return to get him. He should sleep, I thought, as long as possible.

Louis-Baptiste and I each carried a suitcase to the car and then returned for the trunk. Carrying it together we descended the stairs. On reaching the ground floor, we crossed the small circular central hall in order to turn right and pass through the bar, the dining room, and the kitchen to the back door. Neither the hall nor entrance were lit but light was shining from the reception, directly across from us. Its doors were closed. To our left, at the front entrance, the dim form of a man could be seen through the internal glass doors.

Within the first foyer of the hotel entrance, there stood a shadow. It had erected itself beside the door, as still as the wall of ancient stone behind it. Facing the opposing wall, the shadow looked as if it were standing at attention, waiting for an officer or dignitary to walk by. Gruff voices rumbling from reception froze my legs and mind with a wild fear. It was the fear of the hunted.

I found myself, with Louis-Baptiste, shuffling hurriedly across the dark of the central hall. We stumbled into the blackness of the dining room and tore through the kitchen, opening the back door slowly. Again we faced the dark car, idling in the alley. We looked at each other in silence and threw the trunk in the back of the car. Inside, we crept forward and stopped amidst the tables of the dining room.

The white linen covering the tables glowed with a dreamlike light. The doors to the reception were no longer closed. The night porter was not there. Neither were the gruff voices. The shadowy form behind the front door had also disappeared. There was only the silver ring of silence stretching behind the dull drumming of my heart in my ears. I recoiled into the darkness: booted feet were punching resolutely down the stairs. Two stiff uniformed shadows appeared in the lobby and jogged out the front door. The floor was empty. We fell to our knees and Louis-Baptiste seized me by the arm. I reeled in terror. I knew what this was: he had come for me.

But Gilles Alain was in my bed.

My mind ate emptily at itself; my body screamed with hatred and fear. I tore my arm from Louis-Baptiste's iron grip and found myself running with a peculiar combination of madness and stealth up the stairs. Something stopped me short. I did not recognize it until a moment later: steps, again resolute and now unhurried, descending from above. Someone was coming. The antique wood of the stair creaked as the feet treaded down the threadbare red carpet.

I stood on the stair as if riveted in place. I listened and took a step forward, and then stopped again. The closer the descending steps approached, the more I was locked in place. Death had finally caught me. I should have died in the camp anyway. . .

Time became fine-grained and spasmodic. I awoke: torn open from within and released from a cage, I turned, leapt down the stairs, and flew back into the dining room. Louis-Baptiste was still there, in the same position, panting in the darkness. I dropped again into the black silence beside him. The steps continued and stopped at the bottom of the stair. Louis-Baptiste and I strained forward. My chest swelled. My hand seized Louis-Baptiste's arm. I could not control my breathing, which was wild and heavy and seemed to me as if it were echoing in the darkened room. A minute passed. Then another minute passed. The steps resumed, this time clapping harshly on the tiled floor of the central hall.

Moving at half speed as in a dream, a man floated into view like some magician's assistant lying on a bed of air. The top of his head was split open, only minutes before struck without mercy by a heavy instrument. Black blood spurted irregularly from the wound and splashed without sound onto silver tiles. Upside down, hanging, bouncing, as he drifted forward: his face. He was wearing my navy English dressing gown, its gold piping slicing savagely at the night. A limp arm hung in the darkness. A twisted finger pointed to the earth beneath the cold tiles. His mouth was wide, frozen in the bizarre laughter of a permanent scream. His eyes stared out into space, like two voids consuming the entire world.

Gilles Alain, slain. Gilles Alain held in delicate talons, a predator's fresh kill. Gilles Alain in the arms of Theodor Dannecker.

I might have screamed. The German officer's face was like animated stone. His lips parted widely in a dysmorphic expression that was both grimace and grin. Exposed teeth ground at his mouth in a convulsive, spasmodic pattern. And like the echoes of his boots in the hall, his face, his terrible face, faintly mirroring the frozen expression of that held by the lifeless body in his arms. Dannecker's face — freakish, inanimate, illumined from within by a dark light. As he walked, he gazed into the porcelain sky of Gilles Alain's exposed chest as if seeking to draw from it life with which to feed himself.

Dannecker and his prey passed to the center of the lobby before us. It might have been a stage. This might have been a performance. With a liturgical pause, Dannecker turned left, and processed, with the same terrible monotony, with the same heavy, resolute movement as on the stair, toward the front door. Gilles Alain's contorted face continued to scream at me as he floated away.

Reaching the far end of the lobby, Dannecker turned and, with his back against the hotel doors, lifted his gaze from Gilles Alain and stared out of the grey sea that now shrouded him. His eyes reached across the dim hotel lobby into the dark recess of the dining hall. A creeping numbness threatened to suffocate me. There was no distance between us. I rose to my feet.

There we stood, peering into the darkness between us, as still as stone statues in a yard. Spectator and actor, absent in one another's performance, joined by a common hatred in an infinite moment. Empty time. Black time. Just as suddenly as he stopped, Dannecker reanimated and stepped backwards, shoving open the doors with the breadth of his shoulders, his gaze never releasing from its hold the darkness where I stood. The darkness that held me. Gilles Alain's body buckled as it scraped through the internal doorway into the hotel's small foyer. As the first doors closed, the external doors opened by the same means. Gilles Alain disappeared into the night.

14 | THE FLIGHT, AND RECOGNITION

I do not recall what happened next. I remember Louis-Baptiste's hushed scream, desperate, almost murderous, pulling me backwards. Then I was sitting in the car behind the hotel. Then we were moving, Louis-Baptiste beside me on the way to Gare de Lyon. A man that I did not know drove the car.

Paris passed me by like the playing of a silent record. Buildings, dark and old, lifeless, haunting, obscurely illumined; car headlights approaching and dying out as they passed. The sky hanging over the city was dense and oppressive. It was no longer snowing.

Standing outside the car, I looked up at the heavy clock tower of Gare de Lyon; its face was dark. A power outage had dissolved the moon-like circle into the black void of another day's hopelessness. The tower threatened the station beneath it by its hideous, dark stature. It pressed like anger against the hard, cerulean-green light of a sky. I thought I saw it falling. The light which was not yet that of morning. The hand of Louis-Baptiste sliding off my shoulder. Louis-Baptiste weeping at the end of the track.

Our driver stood beside us, a little distance away. No one spoke. A few men in suits of brown or grey stood about, their identical fedoras keeping their brains from spilling onto the station floor. When the train came, Louis-Baptiste and the driver helped load my considerable luggage onto the rack at the end of my car. Sitting in my seat, a dull drum-like horror was beating behind my temples; the cracked red leather of the arm; a woman or a child's yellow scarf, dirty and crumpled on the floor beneath the seat in front of me; my back against the window. I was exposed, unprotected. I lost my breath at the appearing of every person entering the train.

The train lurched forward and began its sad crawl into the night.

There were a few passengers scattered throughout my car. I could not sleep. I could not bear to close my eyes. I handed my ticket to the official, whose droning monotony was only broken by his unambiguous recoil when he looked at me. I stared at him, unable to speak.

A woman, following a small child, walked through my car; they walked back. I wondered if they were looking for a scarf. One man, a few seats away from me was snoring. I disappeared.

I opened my eyes. A man, clutching a soiled paper and muttering to himself, sitting across the aisle to the right. My heart leapt into my throat. I had not seen this man before. How had I missed him? I had not fallen asleep. Had I?

The man's eyes, shifty and anxious, roved the car and periodically passed and then rested on me. Whenever I looked in his direction his eyes would start roving again. I closed my eyes and opened them. He was sitting beside me. "I had a dream." I spoke. Fear shook me. The man stared without blinking. His face was cruel. He was only a face, a terrible unbroken face. His look was one of judgment, of anger, perhaps of terror. As I spoke, the words became the realities they signified.

The man changed. Staring at me, he had the face, now, of a child, of the child.

"In my dream," I tell him, "I was an old man, a dying man." And I am telling a story to a little boy in a room of crowded people.

— Do you understand?

I confess I do not. I only understand death in terms of dream. Or is it life that I understand that way? At the story's end, I breathe my last. It is 1974. I am in Paris. It is a bright day, but its colors, its life, are dull and distant. A warm wind is blowing through the open window of my apartment. Among the people assembled before me are three beautiful young women — my daughters, and a fourth, still vibrant, still beautiful: my wife, decades younger than myself.

They are all listening to me. They think my mind is gone. But it is not true. For there is also another presence in the crowded room, little, vital and quiet, imperceptible except to those with eyes grown dim to this world, those with eyes that open, for the first time and as if newly born, to the hidden world. This little presence stands by a dying man's awkwardly turned head and holds his aged hand. (I know, I am the old man in the dream, but I am also watching, from above.) The old man speaks to this little spark of light, this warmth, this tiny epochal truth as if, together, they are on quite familiar terms. In fact, we had spoken — I felt this, how I feel this! — many times. Perhaps we spoke in the countless dreams I have forgotten when, following the birth of a morning's sun, I crossed the threshold into waking life. Day after day. Perhaps the content of these oneiric encounters is simply too weighty, too ponderous to contain in this waking world, as if one were to try to place a mountain inside of a skull. And what about the entire range of mountains of which that little mountain is only a tiny fragment? And what about the massive, variegated crust of the earth, with its heights and depths, its diverse range of geographical, climatic differences, searing heat, burning cold, darkness and light? And the sun-system, the galaxy, the universe of which such a large mountain is incomprehensibly far, far less than the slightest perceptible point?

I was fathoming these things, gazing into his face, where, like daylight, I recognized something in its features: We, the boy and I, are on familiar — one could say familial — terms. I continued speaking, enchanted by the words, by the realities into which they bled. "The story that is told, as I lay dying, is an ending of sorts. Consider it a bedtime story, told by a father to a son," I suggest to the boy. "But here," I say, "here in the dream, it is the old man who peacefully falls asleep at the end." The little boy whom only I can see laughs. We are no longer in the train car. We are in the words of my story: my apartment, my deathbed, surrounded by faces and wind and light. The boy laughs. And when he laughs it is almost as if the beloved family and dear friends — faces that I knew, faces that I did not know, but they were all dear to me — the dear ones of a worldly man, along with the room, the busy city outside, the spinning world, the sun and stars, all fade into a soft gray, a cherished memory — but a memory nonetheless. But as they fade, and before each of my death-bed visitors silently, mournfully departs to return to his or her ordinary concerns, each one there listens to this whispered story, this story I am telling — the story of a dying, delirious man, with rapt attention, without moving, almost without breathing.

— And the boy . . .

. . . whose cheery eyes flash with the fire of unfathomable

worlds? You! You fill the room and burst through the small confines of the human universe: you will escort this old man, newly born, you will guide me across this threshold into, not the world of dreams, but — as far as we two are concerned — of realities. And then, only then: I wake up.

The shifty face of the man. The train car. Noises, electric light. The man's face opens, his mouth moves in violent, halting gestures. His words send a chill through my body: "We are free, Gilles Alain, we are free!"

The voice was mine, but alien. As alien as the rigid face of the man again seated across the aisle. I cannot breathe...

With cruel suddenness, what happened a few bare hours before replayed before my eyes: the stairs, the feet, the pounding silence of my heart, the SS officers jogging through the hotel, the darkness, the frantic fear — Gilles Alain: his cold blood spilling from the matted wound on his head blackening the lobby's tile floor. The face of Dannecker staring into the darkness, into my soul...

15 | A VOICE, AND TWO EMPTY PLACES

I am dying now. Am I dying, or dreaming? The light is fading. A purple-hued twilight tinges the world of my eyes. There is pain, without a source, without a name . . . And with this pain the many dimensions of existence are caving in on themselves. All around me, all is disappearing. I am struggling with something, someone. It is heavy, oppressive, like the weight of water on your chest when you swim to the bottom of a deep pool. Everything is dark. Is this how it happens, the end? Everything is grey. Everyone surrounding me on this bed has disappeared: my wife, the children, my friends . . . I am stripped of every support. The room, the bed on which I lay, my body — these are all gone. Where are you, my little angel, my child? I can see nothing, but I can feel myself, my being, falling like a stone to the center of the earth. That is all I am capable of feeling. Why can I not see you? Strange forms sit still like statues or are slowly morphing in the darkness. Screaming without a sound, and unable, for a long moment of terror, to pull myself out of the black hands of something vicious, something pressing, a terrible weight on my chest, pinning me down. It is scraping, digging, eating my soul . . . Like a cloud rushing past the sun, paralysis releases me, and my cry translates into a world of waking as a weak, muffled moan. I open my eyes.

My car is empty. The train is not moving. The sun is shining. I am breathing. My chest bears traces of a heavy weight; my arms and legs are lead, difficult to move. I had been locked in a dark dream, but had I slept? I stand and walk to the end of the train and then back to my seat. The train is not stopped at a station but in the middle of a field, somewhere south of Paris. Mountains are just visible in their purple-grey cloaks, resting on the horizon. The train lurches forward. No time passes for me before we approach a station; I think it is Cezy or maybe Laroche Migennes. My heart begins to race: the train must have stopped several times while I slept, for we had passed a number of stations on the line. I did not notice them. What a dream I had . . . It was pleasant. Was it? There was something — I was old, in a bed, there were people . . . I was telling a story . . . not to them, but to him, to you, an angel . . . to my angel. But had I sl——

— *You are whispering* (I cannot hear . . .)

I slump in my seat and slip into a panic, for I cannot remember the name of the station I am to disembark onto from the train. I cannot think of anything. It is as if the black hands of darkness, in their cold grip, drain my waking mind of its capacity to string together any thoughts, to recall anything at all. A creeping feeling corresponds to the hazy numbness of my mind. The dread takes up again its residence in the form of pressure in my chest and head. I feel my face but I do not recognize it. I do not know where I am, I do not know the war, the camp, my escape, my brother and father and mother, my friends . . . my dead . . .

Then I hear it. A voice. The voice of someone loved by me. The voice of Gilles Alain. I hear it in my mind. (Or is it over the train loudspeaker?) He says the name of the station at which I am to get off the train . . . where I am to meet my contact, to be saved, to reach my father and brother. To live.

Now I remember: the train I am on: it is the Paris to Marseille. Marseille on the coast: where I was born . . . This train, it passes through the major cities of Dijon, in the Occupied Zone, and Lyon, in the south. Just north of Lyon the train stops in Mâcon, where my brother and my father are. In fact, Mâcon is the last stop before Lyon. Now I think: why not simply ride the train there? I feel a powerful inertia come over me: if I do not move, then it will not be my action that leads to my arrest and eventual murder. No, it will be the action of others. Perhaps if I sit perfectly still, if I do not look anyone in the eye . . . No, I will look them in the eye, with all confidence and nonchalance, and perhaps then the Germans will pass me by when they inspect the train and check IDs at the last stop before the train passes into free France . . . No, no. I should, I must, follow the plan. Reaching into my jacket pocket I feel something sharp and cold. It is a memory. The tiny screw I found in the holding room at the police station where I spent a night of angst and insight during my transfer from the prison to the camp. The screw that cut my fingers; the blood with which I wrote my confession on the underside of the table . . . The memory, like a stinging insect, flashes through my mind. I place the screw between my fingers, just as I did in that darkness, and squeeze, scraping with all my remaining strength the bottommost dregs of my willpower. I do not stand until the train stops. I look fearfully out the window onto the platform. I see a man, Dannecker, standing there, hands clenched in his brown gloves, flanked by two henchmen with wicked smiles, waiting to devour me.

I look again. My hand slides into the left hip pocket of my jacket, slipping around my Drancy lunchtin. It comforts me.

— *Despite yourself, you live.*

The platform is empty.

I descend onto the platform and stand. My luggage! Gesturing at no one I leap back onto the train and see the two suitcases and small trunk wedged together in the luggage rack. I pull at the handle of the second suitcase. It does not move. The weight of the trunk on top of it holds it fast. I begin pulling at it frantically, pressing my foot into the suitcase below for leverage. The suitcase does not budge. I reach for the trunk, but there is no handle with which to grab it. My shaking hands slip along its sides. I cannot dislodge the trunk from the rack. How had Louis-Baptiste placed the trunk in this luggage rack in the first place? It is as if the rack were built around the trunk. I decide to leave my luggage behind. Turning around, I freeze: in the doorway of the car is a man, observing me. A German officer. He is large, a terrible statue of darkness framed by the light outside the car. I cannot see his face; there is only the terror when I see his uniform. The branches of a green tree wave in the bright distance behind him. Where did he come from? He animates and approaches me. I step backwards and hold my hand up before my face. He pushes me to the side. Without a word he grabs my trunk, turns it slightly and rips it from the rack. He exits the car and then returns. Pulling my two suitcases down he carries them out of the train. I follow. Standing beside my trunk with the two suitcases stacked on top of it, he waits for me. Surprising myself I say, with a courteous affection: "Thank you, sir." He says nothing, turns and disappears off the platform.

I leave the suitcases and trunk just as he had stacked them and move unsteadily to a painted wooden bench along the wall. The platform is deserted. It is cold, but the sun is shining. I sit in the shade and shiver. An hour passes. There are no sounds. No birds, no trains in the distance, no wind. Silence. No one at all appears. I walk over to my luggage and stand for a moment before returning to the shaded bench. The station is nothing but a small covered platform of steel and painted wood. From my position I can see no buildings, only forest and hills in every direction. As every minute of the platform clock ticks forward, my alarm grows. Am I in hell? Perhaps I myself died at the hands of Dannecker. I look back to last night's events in my mind's eye: I am the one carried in Dannecker's arms. I am screaming silence, paralyzed death. I see myself staring at me from the dark across the hall. I feel the weight of worlds falling all over me. An hour passes. Another hour passes — so the station clock says. Something has gone wrong. Where is my contact? What am I to do?

16 | A SOUND, TWO CARS, MY FEET

The ticking of the station clock ceases. A sound. There is a car crawling up the road behind me. I leap to my feet. The car stops. A door opens and shuts. I dare not move. Is it the German officer returning? I conclude that my contact has run into some trouble and that the plan has fallen apart. I wait for fate to decide. A tall, strangely thin man climbs into view. He is wearing wide black slacks that, despite his height, appear too large for him. A dingy sports jacket hangs halfway down to his knees. He quickly crosses the expanse of the deserted platform and approaches me.

He asks, "Is this Professor Wahl?" His forehead, cheeks and the end of his nose are red with sunburn.

"How is that possible in the winter?" I ask myself.

"Is this Professor Wahl?" he asks again.

I feel as if he is speaking to someone else standing next to him, someone I cannot see.

Then, without waiting for an answer, he turns and faces my luggage, directly addressing me now, "Do these belong to you?"

I look around at the empty platform. When I respond with a meek, "Yes," he grunts, mutters to himself, and grabs the two suitcases, placing them on the platform. With a heave, he picks up the trunk and walks to the car. I grab the suitcases and struggle off the platform behind him. He returns, rips them from my hands, and lumbers them down the stairs.

I walk around the running car and sit in the front seat. He says nothing. We drive off. He does not speak unless I ask him a question, and, even then, half of his responses are mumbled so softly that I cannot understand him. I do not know why, but I am afraid to ask him to repeat himself.

We drive for an hour, always — the best that I can tell — south and east. I understand nothing about this man, except that he seems to be suffering from something. He makes me feel uneasy. He does not belong in this setting, like a sunglassed man with a towel and bather's trunks walking across a scene from an American Western film.

We finally reach a deserted crossroad. A car is waiting with its windows rolled down. The motor is not running. The tall man and I ease up behind and emerge from the car. A man steps out from behind his car. How had I not seen him standing there? He is small, wiry and wears an old once-red Phrygian cap. He wears thick mud-brown wool pants cut off below the knee, a matching shirt of the same material, and a vest of a lighter color but still of the same thick wool. He resembles a peasant in his Sunday clothes. The tall man introduces me, but without trading any names. I get in the car. My new driver is already sitting in the seat.

As he starts the car I shout: "But my suitcases!"

The tall man, standing just outside the car, snaps back, this time as if the suitcases are his own. He says, in the first person: "What about my suitcases? We will get my suitcases. I may have to run for it yet."

I stare at my feet, pressing through the soles of my shoes into the floorboard as the earth begins to race away beneath them.

17 | ANOTHER DRIVER, AND WE STOP

My new driver is talkative but he speaks of nothing: the weather, the end of the war, the peculiar character traits of children. He speaks of everything animatedly, but also as if it were dancing far away. We drive for an hour and as we drive the sky darkens. Again, we proceed south and east, this time along roads that are even smaller than the first. I do not think we see another car, but several times we pass people in pairs or alone on foot. We finally approach another crossroad where there is a car waiting. A short, brawny man stands beside the car, his arm resting on the door. His sleeves are rolled up and his arms are covered in thick, curly red hair. He is preoccupied. Without a word I get into his car and we start off. I speak little. He speaks in monosyllables.

We drive through the darkness until we reach the little village of A———. In the middle of the village the man stops the car and jumps out. He runs into the *bistro* across the street. I imagine him stopping for dinner while I wait in the car. I laugh mechanically. He comes back out after a few minutes and sits again in the driver's seat. Without looking at me, he says that I will have to spend the night in the village. The plan is to get me over the border tonight. "Except that, forgive me, German patrols are operating in the area." He speaks as if this might have been his fault. He drives to the end of the street and turns right, stopping before a small row of houses tightly packed together.

18 | A DECENT GLASS OF PORT

The door of a well-maintained house at the end of the row is opened for us. The man in the threshold is diminutive, a little smaller than I. Behind him stands his wife, the four fingers of her right hand raised to her opened mouth in an involuntary expression of shock or concern and helplessness. For the briefest moment, the faintest touch of her tongue's pink flesh appeared through her parted lips. Living flesh is so delicate, vulnerable. Her face is beautiful, but her expression is ugly, like a child who in her innocence has not yet learned that a certain unwitting expression displeases adults. Danger like this will unmask even a French woman's careful concern for self-portrayal.

The man at the door first gives the appearance of being well-to-do; his wife gives the appearance of being even more well-to-do; the man speaks with a nervous stutter; his wife speaks quietly and swiftly, as if by every word she is endangering herself. She is a little bit larger than he in stature, with wavy blond hair. But she is not plump. In fact, she is neither plump nor thin, but rather fleshy and big boned. Yet she is not large, nor even middle-sized. She is small. Neither of them seem prone to laughter. The impression of their wealth comes from their serious and noble manners. But their home is not elegant. Nor is it impoverished. They wear the cares of the world — or at least of this war and of their courageous choices within it — on their faces. A large crucifix hangs on the wall behind them. A small wooden font, dry of holy water and very old, is stationed just inside the door.

After he closes the door the man slides his fingers into the font out of age old habit. He does not make the sign of the cross. Their sitting room is filled with simple wooden furniture. The house is clean and not comfortable — although not uncomfortable. The fireplace to the left is burning with a small fire. A narrow wooden stair rises to the right. Through the doorway is the kitchen, which is, again, simple and clean, with a heavy, square wooden table. Without ceremony they lead me back through the open doorway into the kitchen.

The table is set for three. A strangely ornate and out of place oil lamp is burning in its corner. The kitchen is warm. The woman immediately serves dinner, which consists of *soupe à l'oignon* in wooden bowls that we eat with slender wooden spoons. In the middle of the table is a large *baguette de pain*. The man says a traditional blessing before breaking the bread in his hands. Giving me one half of the bread, he tears a large piece from the other half and passes it to his wife. We eat the soup, speaking almost in hushed whispers. Our conversation is warm but also hasty. They are not at ease with the situation. Neither am I.

After supper the man opens a cabinet and pulls out a bottle of port. He pours two glasses and gives one to his wife. "Professor, would you like a glass?" I nod, and he fills the second glass further, nearly to the brim. He hands it to me. His wife drinks the port in small sips in quick succession, never lowering the glass from her lips. She finishes the glass before I lift my own. But it is, in fact, decent port: a tawny, both nutty and sweet. This man and wife sit at the table in silence. There is no cheese. A car crawls by outside; they exchange weary glances and shift in their chairs.

I hurriedly drain my glass. The woman stands and begins clearing the table. The man takes me to my room, upstairs, the first door on the right. "This room," begins the man, "is my son's . . . He is a soldier, a prisoner of war. I think he is in Germany."

19 | WAITING

I t is evening. The triple glass of port washes me into a dreamless sleep. I am awakened at dawn as if at the very moment I drifted off to sleep. The woman is knocking on the bedroom door. I am not rested; neither am I tired. I am lying on my back on top of the bed, in my clothes. My shoes are still on my feet. I could have been sleeping for a moment or an entire day. I wake to a nightmare, fearful less because of its terrors, which seem distant, although perpetually coming for me, and more because of its bizarre monotony. She cracks the door and tells me that breakfast is ready at my convenience. To her surprise I stand up and follow her downstairs.

A second *baguette de pain* is on the table and the wooden bowls have returned to their places. The woman pours black coffee into the bowls. The man says the same blessing and breaks the bread just as before, passing me one half and breaking the other half in two before passing it to his wife. This time the bread is hard and a little stale. The woman breaks the bread into tiny pieces and drops them one by one into the hot coffee. Then she picks up the bowl, drinks its contents and eats the remaining soggy bread with her wooden spoon. The man holds the bread in his hands and dips a corner into the coffee, watching the liquid absorb into the bread. He bites off the saturated piece and places the end of the bread into the bowl while he chews. He eats the bread this way until it has disappeared. I do not taste the bread or coffee, only seeing that my bowl and plate have become empty.

After breakfast, they move me into a chair in the sitting room. A new fire is prepared in a clean fireplace. The man appears again and lights the fire. He and his wife wander about the house, speaking in whispers as they pass one another, leaving and returning to the window beside the door to peek through its drawn curtains. They were sage green. I look at the ceiling and then at my feet. They are both still. The man sits down, smiles, and begins a conversation about either the resistance in France or improvements to the metro system in Paris (I cannot remember). Then after an awkward, agitated silence he jumps up, rushes to the window and glances through the curtain. His hands are trembling.

20 | WATCHING

The fire crackles and pops and dims. I hear the clock on the church bell tower sound ten. A few minutes later there is a light rasping at the door. My host jumps up. He opens the door. I am standing by my chair. The previous day's driver enters and stands before us. There is no car this time: he has come on foot. He is wearing the same clothes as before, though his sleeves are no longer rolled up above his elbows. We stare at him for a moment before he quickly closes the door. He does not acknowledge my presence. The woman is standing in the doorway to the kitchen. The fingers of her left hand are raised to her chin below her parted lips in the same manner as when I came to the door the evening before. The man and my driver speak hurriedly, almost at a whisper. I cannot make sense of what they say, although I am not far away. I only pick out a few names that mean nothing to me and the words "patrols" and "fucking Germans." They open the door and leave together. The woman comes to tend the fire, which has been left since the man started it. She places a small log on nearly extinguished coals.

About half an hour later the man returns alone. "Everything," he says, "is arranged." His wife appears from out of the kitchen, where she has evidently been sitting, silently, and perfectly still, since he left. When I see her, I have the feeling that she has been praying. They both sit down in the matching cloth-covered wooden chairs to my right. Together we gaze into the fire now raging in silence. The woman rises and puts another log on the fire. The flames surround the log like supernatural love or wrath. The flames leap up into darkness above them with the force of the longing that seethes at their center. The fire threatens to consume the fireplace. The woman, the man, myself, the house are all absorbed by the flames. I do not know the passing of time. When, as if awoken from a dream by the very act, I raise my head to speak (I am going to ask him what, exactly, had been arranged), the man jumps up and runs to the window and, halfway there, returns without looking out. "We can only wait now," he says.

The clock measures out eleven strokes over the town.

21 | THE STENCH OF PIGS

With the last stroke of the bell still bleeding in the air, we hear a car draw up to the house. By the sound of its squeaking breaks, I determine that it moves, stops, and then moves a little more. The engine remains running. Neither the man nor the woman move. After an awkward delay, they tear their gazes from the fire and look at me. I know my time has come. I open my mouth: "What do I do?" The woman turns to her husband. He rises and moves to the window. He gestures to me to come stand next to him. I obey and peek through the opposite side of the curtain. Outside is a rusty red butcher's van. The front doors, set directly above the wheel well, are painted tan. The wheels are painted red. On the side of the van, against a white background is painted the profile of a pig. Below is the name of a butcher in flowing script: *Simon Lelouche*. And then underneath: BOUCHERIE. We watch for some time. Nothing happens. Without warning, the driver opens the door and leaps out of the van. He is young. He wears a thick grey sweater and a grey cap. He walks to the back of the truck and opens the double doors.

"Ne-ne-now! Quickly!" shouts the man. His voice rings painfully in my ear. Dazed, I look into his face. His eyebrows are raised and his mouth is open. His eyes leap out of his skull at me. I cannot comprehend his words. I hear them, I know what they mean, but the potent animation of his face and the force with which he has yelled them overwhelm me. He pushes me to the door and opens it. I look out at the young man, who is looking back at me. He is unmoving. There is no command, no will or intuition. I fly out the door and down the short brick path to the van and leap through the open doors onto a pile of dirty meat sacks, stiff from the cold. The meat sacks are empty, but the van smells of beef and pork. The doors shut me into the darkness of the world.

The van lurches and clambers down the road. It turns and continues and turns again. A tiny slit window opens above my head. A thick ray of light shoots into the back of the van. I open my eyes and roll over. I can see my driver's chin through the slit as I sit with my back to the metal floor beside it. The van hums along.

"Where are we going?" I ask.

He begins his explanation. His confident youthfulness strengthens me.

"Our destination is a farmhouse, Monsieur Wahl. It is remote, every bit as far from one village as any other. This farmhouse is most conveniently located . . ." he coughed and cleared his throat, "for enterprises of our kind."

The stress he places on the words "most conveniently" and "enterprises of our kind" gives the impression that, in speaking to Monsieur le professeur, this obviously intelligent but provincial lad feels less awkward speaking in extraordinary phrases with a ring of the big city about them.

He continues, "The front door, you see, Monsieur, is in Occupied France, but the back door, ha ha!, is in the zone libre! We have smuggled a number of fugitives — Jews, communists, a resistance fighter or two, yes? — into freedom. In about twenty minutes I will pull up and park the van in front of the house. When I open the doors you will walk to the front door, open it, proceed through the house, at your own leisure, and through the back door. Et voilà: you are home! You are home, I mean, by going through a house to the other side! Isn't it funny? Yes, you think so . . . If I were you, I mean, I am glad I am not you, but if I were, I would pour myself a large glass of milk — they have cows on this farm, you see! — and take a nice long break at the kitchen table before leaving the house to get home. And then you will never see me again." He pauses and states matter-of-factly: "It is as simple as that."

"As simple as that? And you, young man, tell me about . . ."

I could not complete the sentence because the young man interrupts me:

"Oh, merde! I wonder what this is."

The van rolls to a stop. The sliding door through which we talk is closed and the world again goes black. I hear the young man lowering his window. A voice appears. I can feel the fear that carries it.

"You cannot go any further," it says. I strain to transcribe into meaning the rattle of words. "It is too dangerous: the Germans have taken possession of the farmhouse. He is arrested. The farmer, his wife is missing — perhaps she fled or the Germans have taken her for . . ."

"C'est des conneries!," exclaims the young man. There is a noise. I imagine him hitting the steering wheel with his hands.

"But listen! They are very close!" There is urgency and even fear, an awareness of an imminent threat in the voice speaking these words.

I crawl out from under the meat sacks. I am still afraid, but I act with resolute obedience to what comes to meet me.

22 | RUNNING

The back doors of the van swing open. As my eyes adjust to the light, I see a man — the man who stopped the truck — standing in the sunlight. His dark eyes are fixed on me; his fists and teeth are clenched, and his arms are raised from his sides. The sun is breaking from behind the row of trees over his left shoulder. His figure darkens. He says nothing. I stumble out of the truck. He breaks into a wild run. I follow. We cross the small ditch beside the road and leap over a low stone wall onto a brown field whitened by a thin layering of frost.

The field looks as if a comb, dipped in dull white paint, has been carefully drawn over its brown surface.

In unison our feet are crunching over the layer of frozen stubble dappling the field, sticking intermittently into the mud beneath it as we run. Reaching, ahead of me, a narrow line of frosted trees that break into the middle of the field, my new guide passes into the trees. His feet enter the silence.

The dormant branches ahead are wrapped with a thick layer of ice.

I struggle to keep up with my guide. Moments later, I, too, plunge into the trees but just as quickly pass through them and back into a bare, muddy expanse.

There is another tree line far in the distance, and in front of it, at the edge of the field, a matching low stone wall patterned with shrubs and a few old trees, and beyond that, softly rolling hills of fallow land.

The man, who is about twenty paces ahead of me now, has bended his path slightly to the right, away from the thin line of trees, which are no protection anyway. He turns erratically, stumbles backwards, and waves me on with a gesticulated urgency, stumbling again. He freezes for a split second and takes off even faster than before. As he runs his head jerks intermittently over his left shoulder. I wonder if he is running from me. I finally realize, with horror, he is not looking at me, but beyond me.

Behind me.

I lurch forward. Reaching the place where he had paused, I, too, look back towards the road. I, too, stumble. I fall to the ground. Catching myself with my hands on the frozen earth, I turn my head again to look back. What I see shoots through me, convulsing my entire body with animal urgency: a green truck, partly armored, partly covered by tan canvas, sitting behind the butcher's van. Two soldiers approach the van. I cannot see if the young man is still in the driver's seat. The soldiers do not see us. I stand back up, hands burning with pain. Motored by wild fear I take off with renewed vigor after my flying guide, who is already — or so it feels — unreachably far away. At any moment, I am sure of it, I will be dead in mid-stride: a rifle shot ringing through the air will reach the dead drumming in my ears as I fall to the frozen ground. Ahead of me the man has tumbled over the stone wall. He reappears, descending the slight slope of the uncultivated field beyond it. His bobbing head and shoulders disappear into the earth. If I stop and turn, maybe they will let me have a cigarette before they shoot me . . . I can see myself: back against a wall, stiff arms raising open hands to their pointing rifles, my silvery breath appearing and fading in the cold air before shots ring and my body slumps to the ground.

Time slows to a crawl in inverse proportion to the urgent anxiety that drives my legs and arms. I press forward. My lungs are scalded by the freezing air that strains with cyclic fury into my chest. I feel my Drancy lunchtin beating, rhythmically, then erratically, against my hip. It is like an angry pagan drum, urging me on. All I see is the wall. It is shaking. The earth on which it sits dances about. The wall is laughing like a hysteric. With every lunge forward I do not get any closer . . . And then, like a contradiction, I am upon it. Without breaking stride I leap over the piled stone, headfirst. As I descend, time accelerates. In front of my flailing arms a large grey rock is set into the ground. The rock flies up at me and flashes, filling my entire field of vision. All is dark.

23 | WAKING

I awake. I am stretched out on the earth. I am lying on my back. The earth's stone coldness drains slow surges of warmth away from my body. My hands and face are numb. A dark tunnel gives way to the plain blue daylight of awareness. A faint pain sprouts and grows from a single, sharp point at the crown of my head. It thickens and intensifies and spreads in a pulsing fluid motion, sending hundreds of spiny and crooked arms that reach over the surface of my head, neck and face. These spines glow all over my body with a severe sharpness that pounds and searches in rhythm with the heavy, numb pulsing that I feel in my hands and feet. My head shakes with pain; inside my skull there is a tense quivering string plucked violently by my throbbing heart. A faint ringing rattles through my ears. My eyes are open: the enveloping sky . . . it is blue and there are wisps of wind-ragged clouds hanging far above . . .

"Where am I?"

A callous face slowly moves into my field of vision. I see a snarled mouth, spittle gathered in the corners. Dannecker . . . I am finished. The face is speaking. I do not understand this face. Do I? I blink. Gilles Alain, frozen in terror. A mist passes before me. There is no sound . . . I cannot grasp the word of his face . . . my mind roils. I look again into the blank spaces, the limitless grey. The face appears. Again it pierces me. I see.

The face: it is yours now. The beautiful face of innocence, of an eternity, with a gravity too large to be understood. I am only a passive observer to the slow parade of transmorphing meanings that cannot be heard or grasped.

My eyes close and open and close again before the picture show of faces.

"*Monsieur?* Get up, we must hurry — oh, my God — come, get up, are you there? *Monsieur, Monsieur . . .*"

Alien shouts appear in the peripheries, echoes from far away.

The man whom I had been chasing through the field is hunched over me. His face is inches from mine; he is grabbing my shoulders; he is shaking me, wild with terror. He tears me from the earth. I struggle to my knees. The ground beneath my feet slides back and forth like a ship, listing in an uneven sea. I take a step forward and fall to my left. The man, beside me, catches me in his arms.

"Whoa! Steady! Come, now, this will not do . . . Take a deep breath . . . That's it. One foot forward . . . Breathe! Good. Come now: again! Go! Go! *Run!*" My mind struggles to climb out of the darkness that grows and recedes in powerful waves along the peripheries of my vision. A few more deep breaths, however, and the dark nimbus ringing my world fully recedes out of view.

The ground pitches to a heavy stop underneath my feet and I take a few wavering steps. There are more shouts, closer now. Gunshots ring out in the air.

I burst into a violent run. I do not look back.

We descend the slope of the uncultivated field below and run raggedly across two further wide fields. We enter a small wood. Only death will ever stop me from running. My guide no longer leaves my side. I trip and fall twice. He picks me up each time. My hands and knees bleed with sharp anger.

The pain urges me on. I leave it behind as I run. I know it will catch me unless I die. The face of my dead body appears before me, resting forever, no fear to disturb its sleep, no evil to threaten its serenity. My arms stretch out. My feet are crunching through the earth. I want to draw it to myself, to kiss my death, to embrace it. I long for its rest to be mine.

I awake again to myself stumbling in the frozen dirt and ice in the middle of another field. The ground catches me. I look up. My guide stands panting beside me, doubled over, grabbing his knees. His eyes are closed. Wet tears fall to the ground from his twisted face.

We are spent. We can run no more.

The field in which I lie is no different from the several we have run through. I raise my head. On the far side there is a small, paved lane. In the foreground, only a few meters away, I am startled to see, standing, brilliant in nature's stillness, a large grey crane, set boldly against the white-brindled earth. With nature's grace, the crane raises its long beak. Its patient red eye pierces with a wisdom older than humanity, a wisdom that only a beast of the sky may possess.

We gaze, stunned by its beauty. The crane suddenly animates its giant wings and releases the earth from its grip. The pain returns to rivet my head as I stand, chest heaving, breath firing into the air in relentless bursts of silvery vapor. Through the sharp and throbbing weakness that grips my body, I feel a strange and alien smile spread over the surface of my face. It is a joyless smile, non-ecstatic. It is not an empty smile, however. No, what it is dawns on me slowly: this parting of my lips is the bodily manifestation of a purely animal feeling, like the chirp of a bird clutching the treetop after evading the jaws of a cat. And it is finally the smile of knowledge: I understand. We have crossed the border into free France.

EPILOGUES

ALL SEVEN OF MY SUITCASES ARRIVED, IN time, on my brother's doorstep in Mâcon: the four suitcases mailed by Madame David and the three—or rather, the two suitcases and a trunk—left in my first driver's car during my coordinated flight to the *zone libre*. My first driver was right: "You might have to run for it yet." And I have that polite German officer at the station somewhere north of Dijon to thank for these latter three pieces of luggage. Without him I would certainly have abandoned whatever books and papers were in them to an unknown fate.

How I got to Mâcon is a simple and — when considered by contrast to the dramatic events of the previous day — uneventful tale. With my guide I walked to the first farmhouse we set sight on, only another kilometer or two away from where we first came to rest.

To the farmhouse we walked slowly, bearing the weariness of the survivors of some ancient battle, wandering in a foreign land. Once the weight of our fear lifted, another weight, the heavy weight of exhaustion descended on us. We did not speak: I was in too much pain and, besides, there was not much to say. The farmer approached us from behind the barn and, after a few simple and courteous words, led us inside to his table. I felt that he understood everything.

On entering the simple farmhouse, nameless and profound feelings that I had not felt since childhood suddenly invaded and lifted me: the house was filled with the smell of *bouillabaisse*, a rich fish stew that originated from my birth city of Marseille, and which we ate with regularity at home, on Fridays, less in imitation of the Catholics and more because it was obviously a nice tradition. The farmer's wife, a beautiful woman of plain manners and natural strength, immediately poured us both a glass of white Burgundy wine, the name of which I cannot recall. The ancient stone oven was large and took up an entire wall of the kitchen. The fire in it was old and mature. Its radiating heat made my feet and arms heavy and my eyes drowsy. The large cauldron sat in the fire like a fat black Buddha, ready to pour forth graces from its boiling paunch. I entered the house feeling weak and a little ill, due especially, I think, to my head injury. Sitting at the farmer's table, the stew set before me, that dizzy weakness was lifted from my body with the potent steam that rose from the thick yellow broth. As in Marseille, the fish and vegetables were served on a plate beside the broth, and the broth bowl had three thick-cut pieces of stale bread floating in it, each already pasted with yellow, creamy *rouille*. I ate the stew voraciously.

My reunion in Mâcon with my brother, my father and his wife, and with François Houang — who was also waiting for me in my brother's house — was a seamless extension of this experience at the farmer's table. In fact, I can remember precisely nothing between the two events: how long we stayed at the farmhouse, what was said between my guide and myself when we parted, how I got to Mâcon — by car, presumably, but who drove me? — and what happened at the door of my brother's house when our eyes met for the first time. I can only recall the first meal we had together, as if I was transplanted from the farmer's table directly to my brother's. And perhaps I was. There were no words among us: at least, I do not recall any. Just my father's dancing eyes, my brother's understated, faux-distant gaze, and François' guileless, bright grin.

Don't you see how such simple events, the constitutive events of human life, the daily bread of our existence, are so meaningful, so deep, so full of worlds in fact? How silence speaks more and discloses hidden depths of the human soul that words can only veil?

— I know . . .

You are the one teaching me even this by your presence . . . Your silence . . .

Silence . . .

Ah, you could imagine that the story ends here, with reunion, healing, a new beginning, a new life.

But escape to the free zone was not yet a new beginning; it was, like everything before the gates of death — and perhaps like everything here beyond them — only a prologue to a new beginning. The fact is that I stayed but a few weeks in Mâcon at Paul's house. I cannot say what pushed me on; but only that it did. I could not stay still. I was home but far from home. Despite the depth and sustenance of the simple joys of reunion with my family, there was something else that dwelled within me. I carried something, and, whatever it was, a gnawing sense of absence accompanied it and ate away at me. This absence exposed a terrible wound that stung me. And out of this wound of absence emerged the horrible blank face of an emptiness. And this emptiness haunted. In my dreams it took on form and spoke to me: the face and voice of Gilles Alain. Not the Gilles Alain who was alive, but the one who was frozen in murdered death, carried away into darkness in the arms of Theodor Dannecker. I began to heal, physically and emotionally, from the moment that I stopped running in that icy farmer's field. But this healing only created a scar. Underneath this scar was that emptiness that seethed out of the wound like yellow pus. And it grew, took the shape of a human hand shod in cold brown leather. This hand seized me and, though sometimes dormant, has never, never still, unlatched its terrible grip.

◆ ◆ ◆

I open my eyes. I close them again. It is the first days of convalescence in the *zone libre*. I am surrounded by family at my brother Paul's house. I sleep in a small bed in the middle of a large room, beside a fireplace that is kept burning day and night. I think I have slept, without an *intermezzo*, for three days. But maybe it was a week. Food — soup, some bread, coffee — is brought to me, three times a day, as I lay in this bed. Even though my head has stopped hurting, I cannot read. Every time I open a book and pull the words on the page into my eyes, a disorienting heaviness, a palpable greyness descends over my mind. My intelligence goes black as if the system shutdown button is the very act of opening a book.

I can only pray. My prayers, though, are wordless, imageless; they take form only as the aspiration of feeling for communion: *communion with what?* (Did you ask me that question?) I suppose with the Nameless, the Hidden, the One to whom I owe life, certainly, but also the one from whom I seek an explanation or answer for suffering — not of my own suffering, which I accept (I do not know why), but that of others, and of suffering in general and of the evil that tears into human flesh, mutilating it, leaving it damaged, incomplete, abortive.

Did I tell you that, during my flight through the fields, I lost the tiny screw that I pulled from the table, the screw that split my fingers so that I could write my "blood confession" in the police station during my transfer to Drancy? It must have finally worked through the seam of my jacket pocket and fallen to the earth. If so, it is there now, buried in the darkness like a seed in the field. But will it germinate, breaking out from its tiny barrow to bear fruit on the earth? Or will it be turned up by the farmer's plow like the bones of unmarked graves? It will give the earth no nourishment, but it will lie exposed until time buries it again. And again. And again. And if the bones of the dead will rise and be joined to flesh made immortal and united to the eternal God, then that screw will survive the annihilation of the worlds and it will speak the words I gave it that dark night.[*]

I say that in my prayer I am looking for an "explanation," but that just is not it. I do not want words, or demand something I can comprehend, a reason for what happened to me, for what happened to my friends. I do not seek a purpose for the Nazi officer's cruelty, his tormented and incongruous existence. I only carry all of this into the depths of my soul,

---

[*] Because Professor Wahl has now mentioned this event twice, I should say something more about it. Crawling underneath the police interrogation room's table that served as his holding cell until the next morning's transfer to Drancy, Wahl wrote, in his own blood, what he called in an ensuing "conversation" with Dannecker, his "testament" or "confession," which was composed of a few lines from Melville's *Moby Dick*: "The living act the undoubted deed/Strike through the mask/that inscrutable thing." Again, it is worth consulting Part II, chapter 5 (§33) of the story's prequel, *First Born* to comprehend the significance of these lines for Jean Wahl. — W. C. H.

where it is distilled, purified by the crushing, tectonic power moving in the hidden depths of my personality, and there elevated, raised (or is it deepened, descended, intensified?) to the point of transfer into the center of perfect stillness, the pure darkness beyond my existence and at its heart, where I end and the Silence begins, framing everything, pervading it like a breath.

That is what I mean by "prayer," and by "seeking an explanation." There, in that bed, my prayer becomes one with the voiceless words screaming at me from Gilles Alain's contorted face. These are words that speak, if they speak anything at all, a language that transcends us, that we cannot comprehend, but which, at the same time, is a language that comprehends us. And the aspiration that carries these silent words of union with suffering and with God does not burn. It is cool, but it is not distant or calculated. It is cool like the dark roots of a mountain.

I descend, I fall into myself, and there I feel this coolness, this immeasurable gravity and weight, and now I feel it suppress the emptiness that plagues me, shaping it into a round, spinning ball. This ball, I feel, is the world: it includes the planets, the sun, and all the blackness, the vacuum-emptiness that reaches infinitely beyond countless burning suns, with their explosive rise and slow exhaustion that cycles again and again against the changeless background of their empty receptacle. It includes all of time from its origin to its end, which runs like a snake over the surface of the ball, encapsulating the universe and rounding it off into the tiny, slight, fragmentary infinity that it finally is.

And I do not seek solace in this prayer. How can I, for what good would that be? Solace, comfort, consolation seem such paltry things: the entire universe that appears before me does not contain what I sought and felt, what I seek and feel; the reality of my feeling fills it and overruns it, as if it is a torrential stream into which the container of the universe is plunged and quickly filled and overrun. And I recognize, on this bed of fire, that to raise the container of the universe to one's lips, to drink it down to its bitter dregs, is only to garner a slight taste, a taste that is true but which can deceive, like stealing a passing glance at a distant mountain range through a window one walks by, mistaking it, perhaps, for a drawing in white and grey chalk on a flat board. Suffering carried into the inner crucible of that prayer, that contemplative fire, becomes a taste of truth, of "the truth of truth" as the Vedanta says (if I can still use that powerful word, and I am not sure, anymore, if I can. And yet I must). We are free to spit it out in its bitterness, or to swallow it. Does it turn to honey? Only prayer, where the limits of understanding are overcome, as if extinguished like a candle in an inscrutable cavern, and all that remains is the vibrating echo of being, of boundless, relentless being, only prayer of this kind can dissolve into countless points of fading light the screaming face of Gilles Alain that haunts my mind whenever I close my eyes.

— How tired I am. The many voices that echo everywhere . . . I tire so easily now. This is not the tiredness of old age. This is not the tiredness after a day of honest labor or a life well-lived. You do not understand the tiredness that I feel. How could you, little messenger of fire from beyond these gates of spinning worlds? The thinning out of life under the caustic, lidless eye of evil. It is like coldness, the ache of nothingness. The shadow has returned. Do you see it? There, in the corner! It frightens me . . . I am only saved by your bright presence, by your eyes! The fire, the fire: it soothes me. Ah, child, my precious visitor, my host: never leave my side . . .

— How my soul aches now, when I think of him! Gilles Alain. How his face torments this old man, this dying man! But I must continue on, I must awake, for his sake . . . and for yours, too, fiery one. You do not understand this, but I continue for your sake, child. And you — I know this, too! — you, too, must keep the memory. Bind it! Bind it to your outstretched hands, to your forehead, to your side, to the intimate part, beneath your arm. It is a wound that will never heal, this memory. Even in eternity. Only an infinite power, like the creative Breath of God, could transfigure it. But I know that even this transfiguration of such a wound will not erase it. Wounds like this never heal . . .

— How do I know this with iron certainty, yet I struggle, like one of those sick, wandering Jews stumbling through the streets of Paris, to keep lit the wavering candle of faith in God? Until that Day when the marks of suffering, though eternal stains on the hands of God, are in some inconceivable way glorified — *if it comes* — this burden of suffering must be borne. You — I dare to address you! *Even you*, must bear this burden. So bear it in your own way. It is life's burden. We each have to bear this burden on our own, for ourselves and for others. For the entirety of the world. Bear it for me . . .

◆　◆　◆

I saw and felt all of this, all that I say, all this same dark immensity, as I gazed into the fire, covered in blankets, alternately cold, feverish, shaking, and hot, burning, sweating, passing with my mind into the very flames that I contemplated until the oxygen in my lungs combusted and I breathed that very fire itself, bathed in it, burnt to ash and risen invisibly to the sky. I am awake, passing, as an oblation, into the spiritual worlds beyond the threshold . . . Perhaps what I have just said is enough to explain why, as soon as I was able, I left that bed and its fire and took the train one stop to Lyon and revived my connections at the university. My former colleagues would receive me with enthusiasm; the dean would make an official address; I would be formally invited to participate in faculty meetings. I would give a well-attended university lecture on Kierkegaard. The dean would secure for me a small apartment, owned by the university, in which I would be placed, free of charge. I would see François daily. I would even resume teaching: a small coterie of students would gather, weekly, in that apartment. I suppose that making myself busy, replacing the damp, decaying earth of my flesh and the rising fire of my spirit with the basic elements of my life before the war, before Dannecker and prison and the camp, would help me to survive.

Survival means continuing to live, and that is what I will try to do.

Survival.

And that is now my last word, my parting word to the gates of the world: "Survival." I am surprised. Who is not, by death? The story is ending for now. I have left myself in the bed, beside that fire of contemplation. And now, now it is another bed, another awakening, the death bed of an old man. But it is the same dream . . .

Here I am, waking. It is another fire. You.

"Survival . . ." Survival is not forever. Or is it? Death is here. Do not let go of my hand. I will fall into the dark that rushes open below. There is so much darkness. It is close. But somehow, now, its threat is stilled. There I am, asleep (am I asleep?) on my bed, floating away . . . Will I ever see myself again? Will I ever see them again, those surrounding, mournful faces, who fade as I depart? Your smile tells me much. You are the face of death for me? You are the fire. How surprised I truly am. — No, I am not afraid. There is the path. The gates are closing behind us, and the mountain looms above. Arise, child, I am ready. Let us be on our way.

AUTHOR'S AFTERWORD

I
t is a common human tradition that, at the moment
of death, the soul undertakes, quite passively, a review
of its completed mortal life, in its totality. Similarly,
humanity, at least, in many places and at many times and in
many variations, also appears to believe that at the gateway
of death the soul is met by a guide, a spirit-being waiting for
it at the edge of the world into which it has awoken. To this
guide from the spirit-world you (for example) will tell the
story of your life. He does not speak, this angelic being, for
if he did (you get the impression), you would not understand,
and more fundamentally you feel that you would be injured
or even obliterated by the sheer *otherness*, by the power and
gravity of the speech that would emerge from this unfathom-
ably great being. You are grateful that he appears to you veiled,
in a splendor that presses you no farther than the very edges
of your capacity. He is terribly familiar and yet, strange . . .

Many — well, a few, more recent, and European, post-
Christian types of intellectual — have also contemplated the
moment of death; some of these have even concluded that
the experience of death is a strict impossibility. How can you
(again, for example) experience *your non-being*? But if death
happens not to be an annihilation but rather a translation
from one state of being to another, then those ancient traditions I referred to have a chance of obscurely relating some
truth — a truth, like your angel-guide's speech, too heavy and

too large to grasp in itself. Too great, in fact, for our embodied minds to encompass, strictly riveted as you and I are to this world of space and time and matter, of human tradition and natural order, with its safe and comfortable limitations.

And let us recall the lesson of that strange specter whose appearance in Professor Wahl's bathroom mirror during his first night "outside the gates" caused him such consternation. The mind, if I understand what he said (loosely restating an argument from the early pages of the Brihadaranyaka Upanishad, by the way), retains the powers of the sensible organs even when asleep. This appearing of images in the mind is the projection of the world of waking, but who can decide whether the sensory experience of the waking world is not itself also a projection of mind, a dream? Who can determine if the dream world is truly restricted to that projection of the mind based on the waking world's collection of experiences? Who can decide between these two options?

Like the specter, I ask this in all earnestness. The story holds the key, does it not? Only by electing one, whether waking or sleeping, as the basis for the other, do we see them both, but our decision can only be ultimately known as true or false *from a higher vantage place*. Perhaps from that place we will see that both options are equally wrong — and, then, equally right. Whatever one's answer, the mind clearly has the power to perceive the world *as it is*, which is either a pure projection of mind (as in dreams), or an existing field of reality "outside" the mind, existing in pure indifference to mind's perception of it (as in waking). And behind both of these vantages, the mind perceives a difference, then, the difference between reality and appearance, between sight and misperception, between knowledge and error.

The mind has the capacity to see and to fabricate a world for itself, whether in dream or waking life. And who can decide between these options, *except the one on the other side of death*, who stands on the edge of the world seeing it for what it is, beyond both dream and waking? The task laid on everyone, inasmuch as death is laid on everyone, is to undertake the work of passing from illusion to reality, ignorance to awareness, into the knowledge (through experience) of what is. The question that, it seems to me, divides traditions and civilizations is whether that knowledge bubbles up like nature within us or whether it must come, if it is to come at all, *from beyond*, through a messenger. But, again, does the messenger merely awaken us to the truth already there or does he carry to us something utterly alien, something active, something new-making, something we could never realize on our own but is *nevertheless essential*, refiguring our vision and unlocking our understanding of that world and ourselves from beginning to end?

In the twilight gleam of these most difficult thoughts, amidst that ancient double-tradition of the spirit-guide and the soul's life review, what can we affirm about the moment of death? Let me propose just this: the experience of your death will be felt like a memory of the present, and your life lived will be like a dream when you find yourself birthed into that place outside the gates. It may be that dying is, after all, much like waking up — and that the cycle of your life, from birth to death and into a new birth, lived every day through the rhythm of sleeping and waking, darkness and light, is a parable, a story that begins, ever begins, to tell the truth. Perhaps that new beginning that surrounds you every morning *is the truth*.

◆ ◆ ◆

During sleep (in dream) he transcends this world and all the forms of death (all that falls under the sway of death, all that is perishable). On being born, that person, on assuming his body, becomes united with all evils; when he departs and dies, he leaves all evils behind.

> Brihadaranyaka Upanishad, III. 7 – 8
> (Mueller, 1879, 163 – 64)

Finally, since I thought that we could have all the same thoughts, while asleep, as we have while awake, although none of them is true at that time, I decided to pretend that nothing that ever entered my mind was any more true than the illusions of my dreams. But I noticed, immediately afterwards, that while I thus wished to think that everything was false, it was necessarily the case that I, who was thinking this, was something.

> Descartes, *Discourse on Method* (Clarke, 1999, 25)

Man in the night kindles a light for himself, though his vision is extinguished.

> Heraclitus, fr. 48 (Marcovich, 1967, 244)

When the body is still, at rest and sleeping, a man is in inner movement — he contemplates what is outside himself, he traverses foreign lands, he meets friends, and often through the dreams he divines and learns in advance his daily actions.

> Athanasius of Alexandria, *Contra Gentes*
> 31.38 – 43 (Thomson, 1971, 87)

When all people are governed by their own minds, there are a few who are judged worthy of direct divine communication;

thus, although the imagination, active in sleep, occurs according to nature to all equally and in common, there are some, not all, who participate by means of their dreams in some diviner manifestation.

> Gregory of Nyssa, De hominis opificio, Patrologia
> Graeca 44.172B (Miller, 1994, 49)

I believe that a man has a phantom which, in his thoughts or dreams, assumes various forms through the influence of circumstances of innumerable kinds. This phantom is not itself a body; yet, with wondrous speed, it takes on shapes which are like material bodies; and it is this phantom, I believe, that can — in some ineffable way which I do not understand — be presented in bodily form to the senses of others, when their physical senses are asleep . . .

Another man told how, in his own house, at night-time, before he retired, he saw a certain philosopher, whom he knew very well coming towards him; and this philosopher expounded for him several problems in Plato which he had previously declined to explain when asked. When the same philosopher was asked why he had done something in the other man's house which he had declined to do in his own, he said, "I did not do it; but I dreamed I did."

> Augustine of Hippo, Civitas Dei XVII.18
> (Dyson, 1998, 843 – 44)

W. C. HACKETT is a philosopher and writer living in rural Indiana. His theoretical exercises include *Philosophy in Word and Name: Myth, Wisdom, Apocalypse* and *Quiet Powers of the Possible: Interviews in Contemporary French Phenomenology*. He has also translated works from French to English, including Jean Wahl's *Human Existence and Transcendence*. He works at a Benedictine monastery. Learn more about the stories he tells by finding him online.